Mel Bay's

HAWAIIAN UKE SONGBOOK

by Ken Eidson
& Ross Cherednik

1 2 3 4 5 6 7 8 9 0

TABLE OF CONTENTS

Hawaiian Ukulele Styles 5

Tuning the Ukulele 6

The Baritone Ukulele 7

Ukulele Banjo and Tiple 7

Rhythmic Strumming, Hawaiian Style 8

Basic Chords 9

The Hawaiian Vamp 10

Reading Tablature 11

Reading Music 11

Notes on the Fingerboard 12

Scales and scale exercise 13

Rhythm 16

Keys and Key Signatures 17

Special Techniques 18

Melody Techniques 19

Ukulele Songs 22

    Koni Au I Ka Wai 22

    Maunawili 23

    Hilo March 24

    Manuela Boy 25

    My Honolulu Hula Girl 26

    He Aloha No Kauiki 28

    Ipo's Song 29

    Sunny Manoa 30

    Honesakala 32

    Maui No Ka Oe 34

    Liliu E. 35

    Waltz For My Dear 36

    Kuwili 37

    Kuu Ipo I Ka Hee Pue One 38

    Paahana 41

    This Pretty Ukulele 42

    Mauna Kea 44

    Lei Nani 45

    Sweet Lei Mamo 46

Hula for Ken. 48

Ua Like No A Like 49

Lei Ohu. 50

Think Palm Trees. 51

Hawaii Ponoi 53

Aloha No Wau I Ko Maka. 56

Hame Pila 57

Halona. 58

Hiilawe 59

Heeia. 61

Betsy's Tune 62

Sweet Lei Lehua 63

Manu Oo 65

Hanohano Hanalei. 66

Lei Ohaoha. 68

Pulupe Nei Ili I Ke Anu 70

Nuuanu Waipuna. 71

Hula O Makee 72

Aloha Oe. 73

Friend's Lullaby. 76

Wiliwili Wai 78

Pua Sadinia 79

Moani Ke Ala 80

Makalapua, Version 1 81

Makalapua, Version 2 82

Luana's Dance 83

Violeta 84

Pauahi O Kalani. 85

Alekoki 88

Alika. 89

Waialae 90

Akahi Hoi 91

Lei Poni Moi. 92

Sakura 94

Advanced Chords 95

Afterword 107

Alphabetical List of Songs 108

FROM THE AUTHORS

Ross Cherednik: I am a counselor and musician in the Hilo area of the big island of Hawaii. I have lived on Maui. My instruments are ukulele, mandolin and violin; I came to Hawaii from the Pacific Northwest in 1967. My wife Betsy and daughter Ipo are active ukulele players. A second daughter Luana specializes in dance.

This book evolved out of the ukulele lessons I have been giving my family. Once they had mastered beginning chords and strums, there was very little learning materials available to them. I told Ken Eidson about the lack of intermediate level ukulele texts, and he replied, "Let's write it!" So here it is. I hope this book can be a beginning towards filling the gap in ukulele instructional materials.

I would like to thank Ken, whose lively sense of humor, general "akamai" and "aloha" and timely feedback were delightful and greatly appreciated. Especially the timely feedback. Ken gives much to the world of music, which is greatly enriched by his presence in it. Mahalo nui loa!

Aloha pumehana,

Ross

Ken Eidson: This is the latest in a series of several books I have authored and co-authored through Mel Bay Publications. I can truly say, however, that I have learned more doing this book than in any of my other ventures. The main reason for my personal learning is Ross Cherednik, a musical amateur in the most flattering sense: he plays for the love of it! His own research abilities (stemming no doubt from his background as a college math teacher) have helped to uncover much about the ukulele's history and playing styles that is largely unknown on the mainland.

Our book covers a lot of ground, and the serious student will find enough to keep his or her fingers busy for a long time. The person who considers the ukulele as simply a time-keeper in the background of a Hula band will be in for a pleasant surprise; and the musician who is looking for a book that will help demonstrate how the current ukulele virtuosos do their musical thing will need to look no further!

Thanks to Mel and Bill Bay for their support and assistance, as always, and thanks to you, because you bought this book. Write to Ross if you need more genuine Hawaiian ukulele records to listen to, and write to me if you need a tape of this book. In the meantime,

Think palm trees,
Ken

For information concerning recordings of the songs in this book write to: Ken Eidson, 1937 Henly Street, Glenview, Ill. 60025.

HAWAIIAN UKULELE STYLES

The UKULELE is an Hawaiian version of the Portuguese BRAGUINHA that was introduced by Portuguese settlers to the islands in the 1870's. The ukulele was adopted by Hawaii's musical royalty, particularly King Kalakaua. This led to general acceptance by the people. The ukulele was intially used as a rhythmic instrument for accompanying hula songs and dances. Hawaii's first ukulele virtuoso was Ernest Kaai, who mastered complex rhythm patterns and showed the instrument's melodic possiblities. The ukulele was patented in Hawaii in 1917.

Early ukulele greats included Johnny Almeida, Bill Paaluhi, July Paka, and Alapaki Smith. As the ukulele traveled throughout the world, non-Hawaiian players of note also developed, including Cliff Edwards (Ukulele Ike), Johnny Marvin (Ukulele Ace), Frank Austin, Perry Botkin, Lyle Ritz and Roy Smeck.

Solo ukulele took a giant leap forward when Jesse Kalima won a Territorial Amateur Hour Contest at the age of 15 in 1920, playing "Stars and Stripes Forever". Jesse also pioneered the low G string tuning which will be used for some songs in this book. In 1948 Eddie Kamae and Shoi Ikemi pioneered the first all-ukulele act. The "Ukulele Rascals", as they were called, brought a new awareness of the solo capabilities of the instrument. A student of Kamae's, Herb Ohta, is probably the best known solo ukulele player of today. Ohta san, as he is known professionally, plays with the clarity and precision of a true master. Kamae can be heard in his group "The Sons of Hawaii", where his rare solos are models of good taste.

Although it is a relatively recent addition to the musical culture of Hawaii, the ukulele has so successfully bridged the gap between antiquity and the present that though the name is Hawaiian and the chords it plays are Western, its music is truly cosmopolitan.

Technically the ukulele is a member of the guitar family. That is, it has all the characteristics of a lute (a plucked string instrument with a flat neck, with 7 or more frets and a separate peg box), except for the flat body, such as is found with the guitar.

In the early days of the ukulele's popularity it was played in "D Tuning" (B - F#- D - A), but
1st 2nd 3rd 4th
in more recent years "C Tuning" (A - E - C - G) has totally displaced the older tuning among
1st 2nd 3rd 4th
amateurs and professionals alike. This book will be entirely in C Tuning.

TUNING THE UKULELE

There are two valid ways to tune your ukulele in C. The first is the usual "My Dog has Fleas" tuning in which the fourth string is tuned higher than the second and third strings. It is called "High G String Tuning".

The above tuning is used for most of the songs in this book, and it is the usual tuning for straight rhythm playing. Melodically, this tuning has a drawback: you can't play notes lower than middle C, and the fourth string is difficult to use at all in melody playing. So another way of tuning is to lower the fourth string a full octave. Called the "Low G String Tuning", it is written like this:

Most of the songs in this book may be played in either tuning with very little difference noticeable to the listener's ear (though the songs are written in music notation in "Low G String Tuning"), but there will be a few that must be played in the lower tuning, for instance "Manuela Boy" and "Honesakala". We will indicate these songs by placing the instruction "Tune the 4th String to Low G" for your convenience.

The ukulele comes in three sizes that are tuned to C. There are the standard, the concert, and the tenor. The larger concert and tenor ukes and also the ukulele-banjo and tiple are favored for solo playing because of their additional frets and fuller tone qualities.

When tuning your ukulele, use a pitch pipe or tuned instrument such as a piano to give you the proper notes shown above.

Also Fret Tuning:

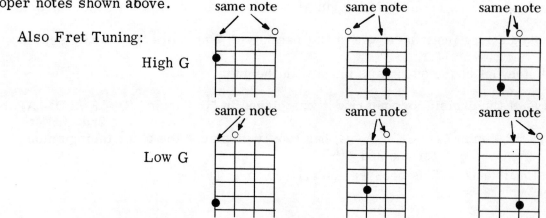

Also Octave Tuning

High or
Low G

THE BARITONE UKULELE

Big brother to the more common tenor ukulele, the baritone uke is not currently very popular in Hawaii, though it may be found in many school music rooms throughout the mainland. The baritone ukulele is generally tuned like the first four strings of a guitar (E - B - G - D), and in

                                                               1st 2nd 3rd 4th

that tuning it can be easily played by any guitarist. The baritone ukulele is not within the scope of this book, but if you have one, you can play out of this book in one of two ways:

1) Using regular Baritone Uke (guitar) fingerings, you can play the notes as written.

2) Using the written tablature (but disregarding the notes above the tab), you can play the songs that way. Using the tab will sound fine, but the songs will be in a different key from the book.

A example of the Baritone Ukulele as a lead instrument can be found in the work of Kahauanu Lake and his trio.

UKULELE-BANJO AND TIPLE

Both instruments are in C tuning, and all songs in "High G String Tuning" can be played on them. Both instruments are still produced, and the tiple is growing most in popularity in contemporary Hawaiian music.

RHYTHMIC STRUMMING, HAWAIIAN STYLE

As a rhythm instrument the tenor ukulele is used in Hawaiian music in much the same way as a mandolin in Bluegrass music or a rhythm guitar in Jazz. It replaces the drums and creates a background rhythm.

The most common rhythm for the ukulele is the CHALANGALANG Rhythm, used in a majority of the Hawaiian songs in the 50's and 60's.

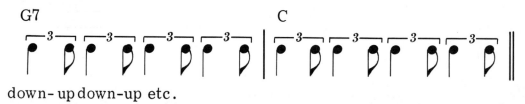

down-up down-up etc.

This works well with "Manuela Boy".

If you have been to Hawaii and seen a nightclub show, you may have seen a musician with a big gourd. He taps it once on the floor and twice on the side, so you have a ♩ ♩ ♩ 𝄾 | ♩ ♩ ♩ 𝄾 | pattern. This is called the Ipu-pahu Hula rhythm, and it is an old style for accompanying Hulas. When this ancient Hula Rhythm is played on the Ukulele it is called the MOLOKAI STRUM. It starts with one strong strum, using all the fingers of the right hand. It is similar to the "rasgueado" strum used on Flamenco guitar. The second and third strums are played short but not chopped. The pattern is repeated throughout the song.

The Molokai Strum will work well with many songs in this book, including "Hiilawe" which is a very ancient song. When you are working out your strumming accompaniments, try both the Chalangalang and Molokai strums to find which fits the particular song.

Ukulele artists often work out their own distinctive strum, based on the standard patterns of Molokai and Chalangalang. Many of these artists are recognizable by their interesting and individual strums they use as a musical "signature". Generally the thumb and all four fingers of the right hand are used on these strums.

BASIC CHORDS

One thing we would encourage everyone to do early-on is to learn higher versions of chords. Basic beginner books tend to give you only open position chords, but it is a very good idea to learn as many alternate chord positions as possible. See the chord chart at the back of this book for more varied ways of playing chords.

BASIC UKULELE CHORDS

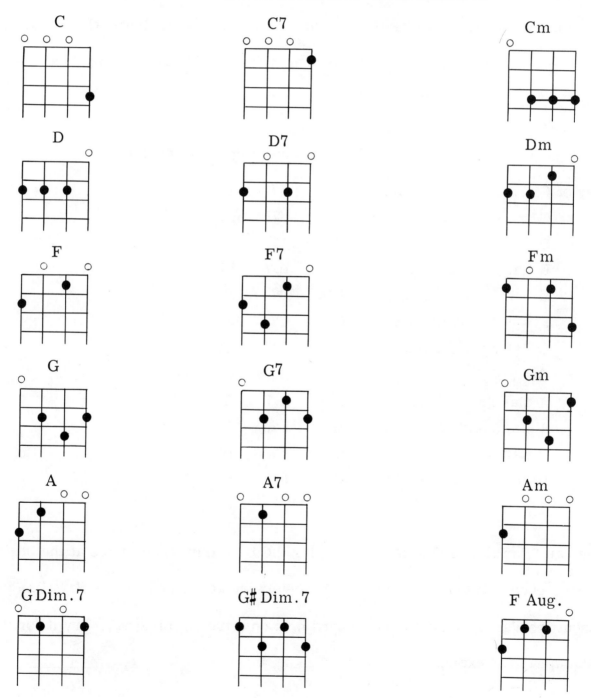

"o" means play the string open

THE HAWAIIAN VAMP

The Hawaiian Vamp is a chord progression used in "turnarounds" (at the ends of verses or choruses, preparing to go back to the beginning) or as a "tag" ending. It consists of the following chords in the key of C: D7-G7-C-C. In the key of G: A7-D7-G-G.

The chord progression itself, called II7 - V7 - I (or V7/V - V7 - I by some musicians) lends an air of authenticity to any song you are playing in the Hawaiian style. In case you would like to know the chords for the Hawaiian Vamp in all keys, here they are.

	Hawaiian Vamp Progression			
Key of C	D7	G7	C	C
C♯	D♯7	G♯7	C♯	C♯
D	E7	A7	D	D
E flat	F7	B♭7	E♭	E♭
E	F♯7	B7	E	E
F	G7	C7	F	F
G flat	A♭7	D♭7	G♭	G♭
G	A7	D7	G	G
A flat	B♭7	E♭7	A♭	A♭
A	B7	E7	A	A
B flat	C7	F7	B♭	B♭
B	C♯7	F♯7	B	B

You can "Hawaiianize" a song by playing the Hawaiian Vamp twice at the beginning of the song, once between each verse, and then twice at the end. Some Hawaiian songs end without the Vamp, using the last chord held on a tremolo instead. Try it for yourself on "Makalapua" for example.

READING TABULATURE

Tablature (or Tab) is a graphic notation which shows you at a glance the string and fret you are to play. We use the four spaces of the music staff to indicate the four strings, and numbers in the spaces to represent frets (O means open):

1st string	2	←— 2nd fret
2nd string	3	←— 3rd fret
3rd string	2	←— 2nd fret
4th string	0	←— open string

Tab is easier to learn than standard music notation, but there is no rhythm indicated by the numbers used in tab. Standard notation can be read more quickly once you have gone to the trouble of learning it. In this book we will include tab for every song, but there will be no rhythm indicated. In order to find out the rhythm, look above the tab to the standard musical notation, where the rhythm will be given with the traditional notes. This may be somewhat bothersome to the individual who is reading tab but not standard notation, but we wish everyone would learn to read music, and this will force the student to study the musical notation in order to get the rhythm correctly. In the process, perhaps some knowledge of the standard notation may rub off.

READING MUSIC

Sharps, Flats (also called Accidentals) and Naturals

A Sharp sign (♯) raises the natural note one fret:

A Flat sign (♭) lowers the natural note one fret:

A Natural is the regular letter-name note, neither sharped nor flatted.
Though not often used, the Natural sign looks like this: ♮

NOTES ON THE FINGERBOARD

The notes on the four strings of the ukulele are as follows:

1st string

	open	1st fret		2nd fret	3rd fret	4th fret		5th fret	6th fret		7th fret

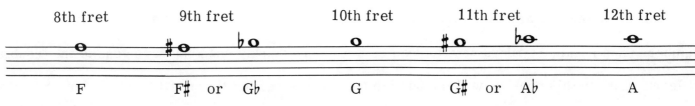

open	1st fret		2nd fret	3rd fret	4th fret		5th fret	6th fret		7th fret
A	A♯ or B♭		B	C	C♯ or D♭		D	D♯ or E♭		E

still 1st string

8th fret	9th fret		10th fret	11th fret		12th fret
F	F♯ or G♭		G	G♯ or A♭		A

2nd string

open	1st fret	2nd fret		3rd fret	4th fret		5th fret

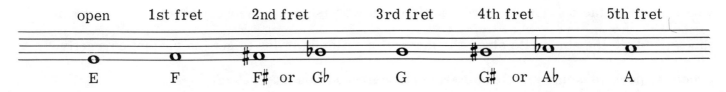

open	1st fret	2nd fret		3rd fret	4th fret		5th fret
E	F	F♯ or G♭		G	G♯ or A♭		A

3rd string

open	1st fret		2nd fret	3rd fret		4th fret

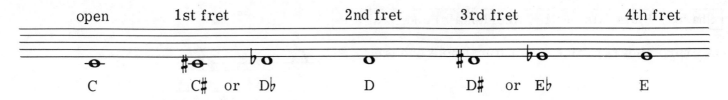

open	1st fret		2nd fret	3rd fret		4th fret
C	C♯ or D♭		D	D♯ or E♭		E

Low G 4th string

open	1st fret		2nd fret	3rd fret		4th fret	5th fret
G	G♯ or A♭		A	A♯ or B♭		B	C

High G 4th string is not used in playing melody notes.

SCALES

Scales are the basis for relating notes to each other in music. Most players use scales in their playing. The following exercise will help you play major scales in all keys and will help familiarize you with the fretboard.

SCALE EXERCISE

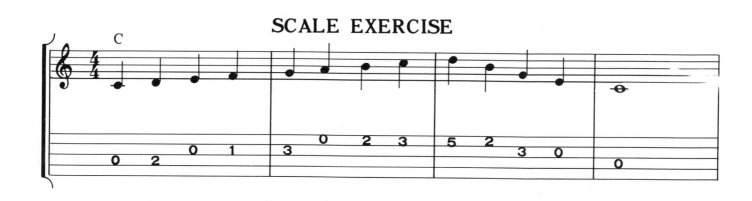

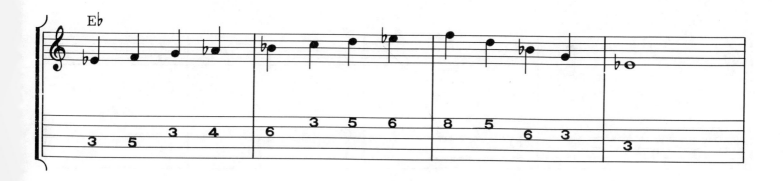

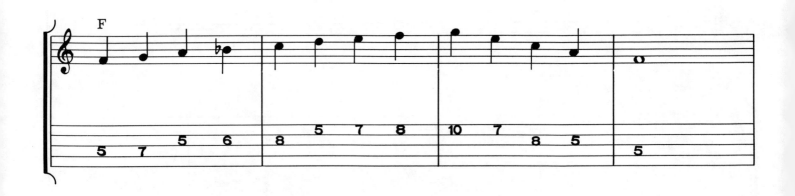
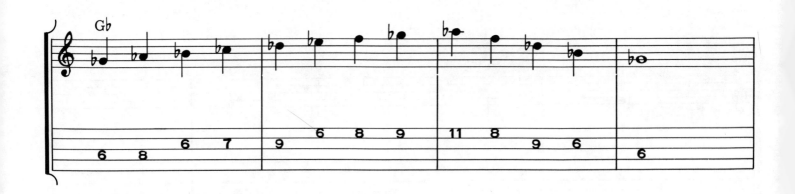

14

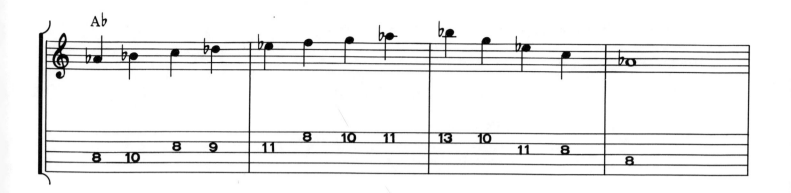

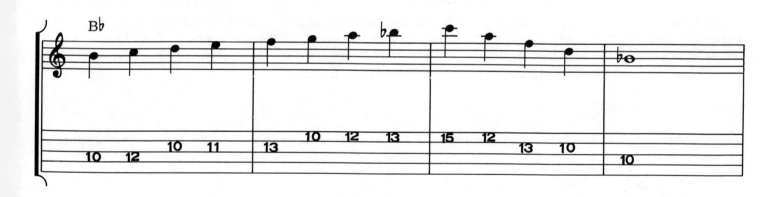

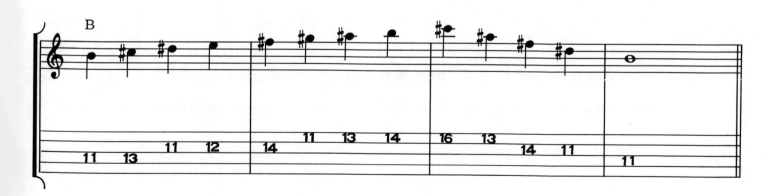

15

RHYTHM

The rhythmic relationship between notes is as follows:

In 𝄴 time,   𝅝 = Whole note = 4 Beats

𝅗𝅥· = Dotted half note = 3 Beats

𝅗𝅥 = Half note = 2 Beats

♩ = Quarter note = 1 Beat

♪ = Eighth note = 1/2 Beat

𝅘𝅥𝅯 = Sixteenth note = 1/4 Beat

Two eighth notes are often beamed together like this: ♫ ; and four sixteenths like this: 𝅘𝅥𝅯𝅘𝅥𝅯𝅘𝅥𝅯𝅘𝅥𝅯

In 𝄴 time, each measure (except for the first measure occasionally, see "pick up" notes, below) should add up to four beats. Any combination of quarter notes, half notes etc. may be used to add up to the four beats. For example:

This example measure
adds up to four beats.

In ¾ time, each measure will add up to three beats.

If a song begins with "pick up" notes that do not make up a full measure, then that measure may have less than the correct number of beats.

Cut Time (¢) actually means ²⁄₂ (two beats in a measure, the half note receives one beat). This is really a speeded up way of reading music. Many fast songs are written in Cut Time so that instead of reading and playing sixteenth notes, you are dealing with eighth notes. That is why we have chosen Cut Time so often in this book. You may work out the songs first in 𝄴 time, and then when you speed it up, you may wish to think of it in ²⁄₂ time.

Rests

Rests are the opposites of notes. They indicate silence. Here are the notes with their corresponding rests:

𝅝 = 𝄻   ♩ = 𝄽   𝅘𝅥𝅯 = 𝄿

𝅗𝅥 = 𝄼   ♪ = 𝄾

Triplets

Triplets are three notes played in the time of two. Three eighth note triplets () are played during the same amount of time it would ordinarily take to play two eighth notes (♫).

KEYS AND KEY SIGNATURES

Keys are group of notes with one note being the most important one, called the Tonic Note. Major and Minor keys are called by letter names. The letter name (for example: G Major) indicates the Tonic Note of the Key.

Key signatures indicate accidentals that must be played in order to remain in the key. The Key Signature appears at the beginning of every line of music as a reminder of which notes are to be played as accidentals.

Some examples of Key Signatures follow:

C Major   No sharps or flats

G Major   All "F's" are sharped

F Major   All "B's" are flatted

D Major   All "F's" and "C's" are sharped

B♭ Major   All "B's" and "E's" are flatted

A Major   All "F's", "C's" and "G's" are sharped

SPECIAL TECHNIQUES

The special techniques used in this book will probably not be new to experienced fretted instrument pickers, but a review of them is in order.

Hammer-on: A note is sounded, and before it dies away, one of the left hand fingers is popped down rather firmly on the same string to produce a second note. The pick is not used to produce the second, or Hammered-on note. Typical hammered-on notes would look like this in the music:

Pull-off: This is the opposite of a Hammer-on. A note is sounded on a stopped string (one on which the finger has been placed), and before the note has died away, the finger is pulled away from the string, producing a second note. Typical pulled-off notes would look like this in the music:

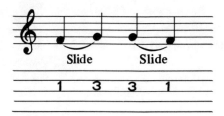

Slides: A note is sounded on a stopped string, and before the note has died away, the stopping finger slides up to another fret. Backward slides are also possible, sliding down to a lower fret. Here are the two slides in musical notation. You can also slide chords.

Picking: Pick direction indications are not given in this book. The rule to remember is that the pick should be alternated up and down as much as possible. You may not always begin on a down-stroke, but the first beat of a measure and any other accented notes should be played with a down-stroke as often as possible. Similarly for finger picking, picking finger is not noted, but the logical choices work.

Tremolo: Tremolo, the fast up and down strokes, should be practiced continuously. The best way to learn a good even tremolo is to play a simple scale or song and divide each quarter note into 2 eighth notes. Later you can divide the eighths into four sixteenths. Always strive for smoothness. After the sixteenths are played smoothly, then work for a faster tremolo. Speed will come easier if your work is smooth and even.

A general rule regarding tremolo is that notes of two beat duration or longer should receive a tremolo. This rule is often compromised for musical effect, so you should always try to use your best judgment on the amount of tremolo to use.

MELODY TECHNIQUES

There are two methods of playing melody on the ukulele.
1) Flat Picking. With a pick you get a rather sharp or
metallic tone. Some players use 8 string ukuleles. A flat pick
is often used on this type of uke.

2) Fingerpicking. Most people start fingerpicking by using
just the thumb. You can rest the fingers at the waist of the
ukulele and pick with the thumb.

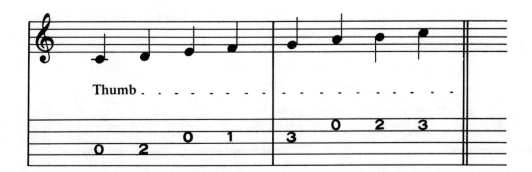

The next step toward increasing you flexibility is to use
the thumb and first finger of the right hand. The thumb should
be used on notes on the C and G strings and the first finger
on the E and A strings.

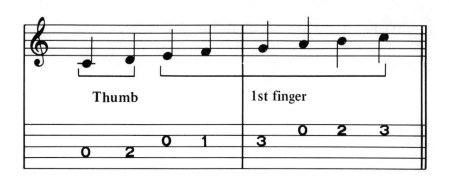

The first finger has a more mellow tone than the thumb. Some professionals in Hawaii grow very long fingernails and play entirely with their nails. They play tremolo by fluttering their nails over the strings.

After playing Thumb and First-Finger Picking for awhile, it's really not too hard to go to Four-Finger Picking (Thumb and three fingers), especially if you run through some chords:

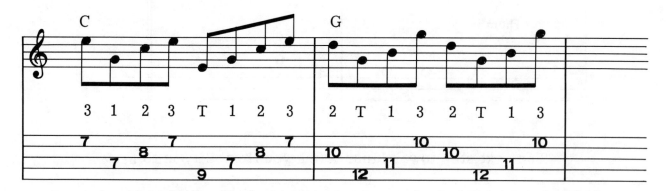

Another good practice pattern to work on is this:

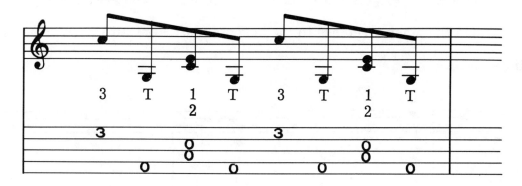

And another common pattern is this:

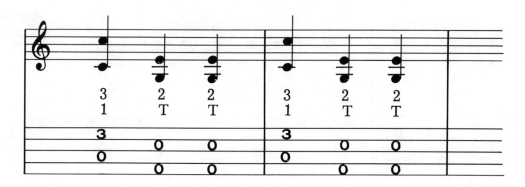

When playing straight melody, using two fingers instead of one gives you more speed. You can also play two-note chords (♩) with either two separate fingers or with one finger. The latter tends to be a slightly more delicate sound.

KONI AU I KA WAI

This lively march can be picked with the thumb or the thumb and index finger. For the left hand, the index finger gets the second fret, the middle finger the third, the ring finger the fifth, and the pinky stretches to the seventh fret. Koni Au I Ka Wai was written as a drinking song.

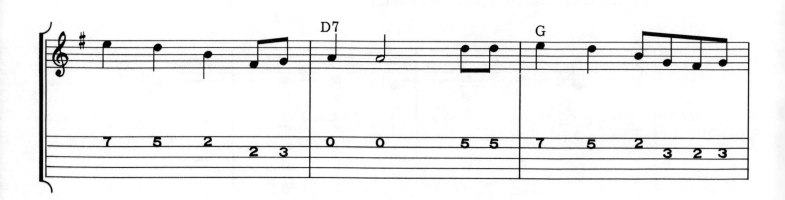

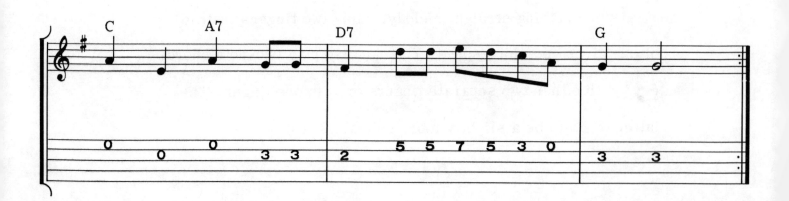

MAUNAWILI

Start this piece with the index finger on the fifth fret, middle on the seventh, ring on the ninth and pinky on the tenth fret. When you reach the A7 chord, shift the index to four, middle to five, ring to seven and pinky to ninth fret. "Maunawili" is based on a Portuguese folk tune.

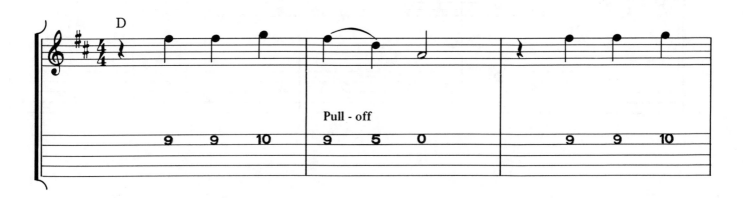

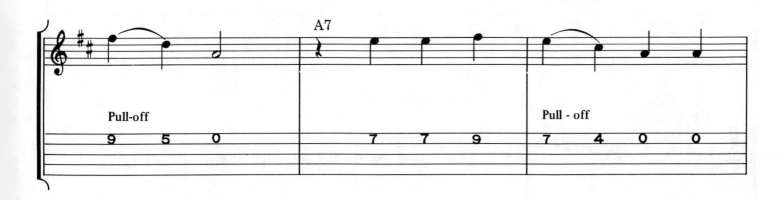

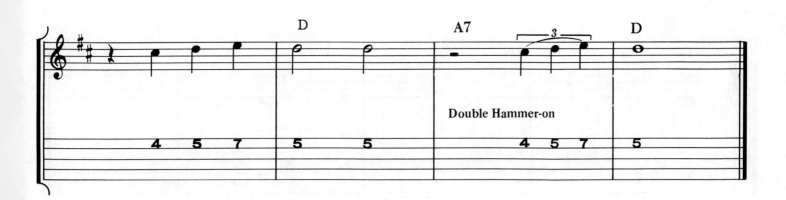

HILO MARCH

A favorite song among steel guitarists, the Hilo March is also considered to be the song of the island of Hawaii. The University of Hawaii at Hilo has adopted it as its school song. It was originally played slowly, but almost immediately it was speeded up. Play it as a lively march. Written in 1881, it was initially called "Ke Ala Tuberose".

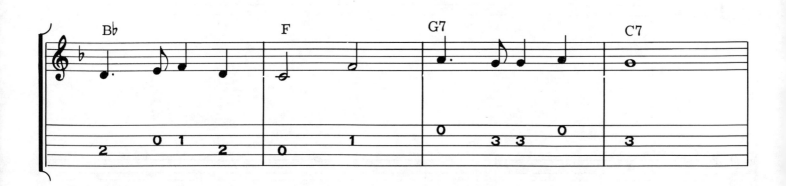

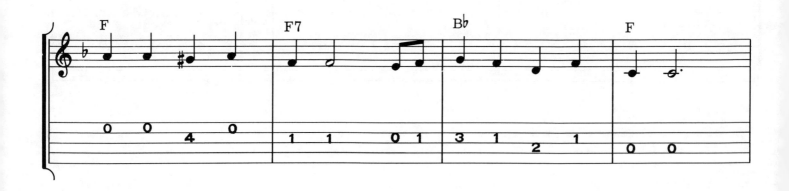

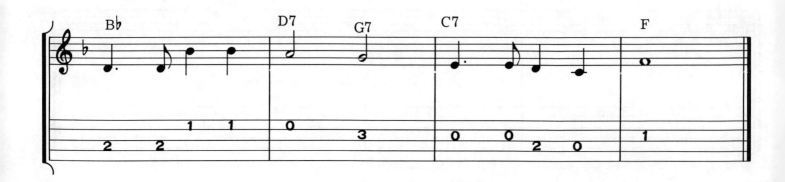

MANUELA BOY

MANUELA is a Portuguese name for a man. The Portuguese were among the first non-Polynesian settlers of Hawaii. They brought with them the BRAGUINHA which later became the UKULELE. This is a common Luau singalong song. This arrangement can be played with a flat pick or with the thumb only.

Tune 4th string to low G

MY HONOLULU HULA GIRL

This song requires Low G String Tuning. The eighth notes can be played either as normal eighth notes or as swing eighth notes. Try it both ways and see what you prefer. This is one of the early "hapa-haole" songs: songs with mixed Hawaiian-English lyrics and a jazzy feel.

Tune 4th string to low G

Verse

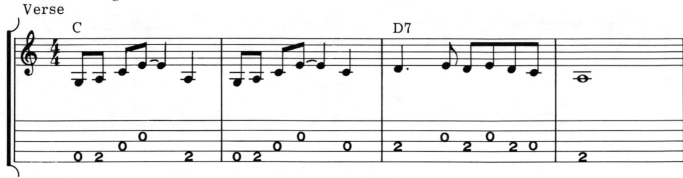

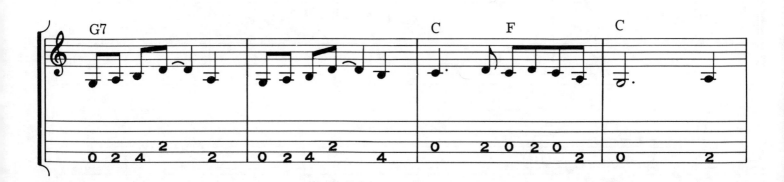

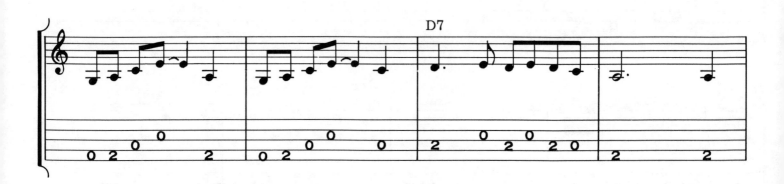

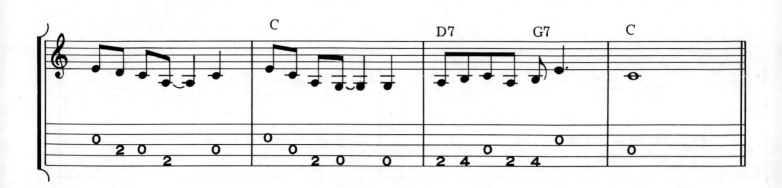

Chorus

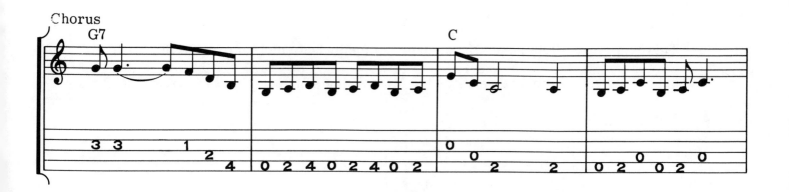

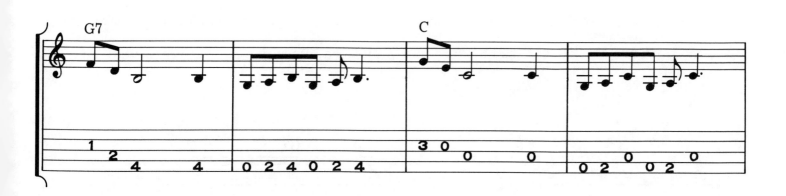

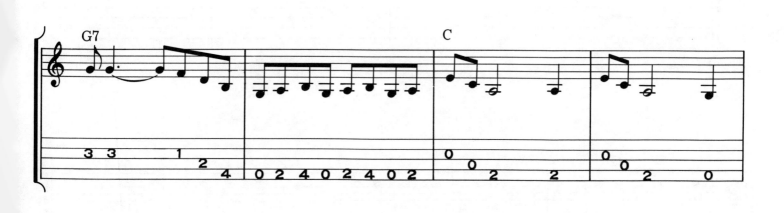

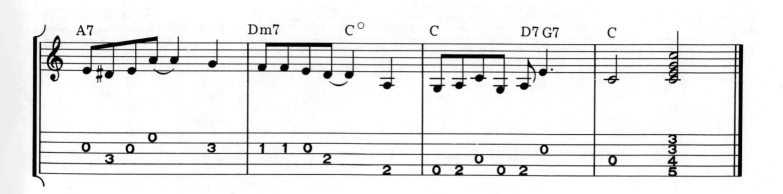

HE ALOHA NO KAUIKI

This is a sitting Hula song. Hand, arm and upper body motion provide the whole story. It should be played slowly and sensitively. Most of the song can be played from one C chord position:

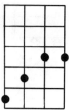

Typically Hawaiian songs are played slower in Hawaii than on the mainland. Older renditions are also slower than modern interpretations. Hawaiian purists resent the "corruptions" of the old songs.

IPO'S SONG

This lively ditty expresses the energy of a young girl. Play it fast as at a playground.

For the A⁷ try:

SUNNY MANOA

This song has many sharps and a few double sharps, which move a note up two frets on the fretboard. Generally the index finger will cover the first two frets, the middle finger three and four, ring finger five and six, and the pinky gets seven. You may find it convenient to alter this rule on occasion.

Manoa Valley is a particularly lush part of the island of Oahu. The University of Hawaii has its main campus there.

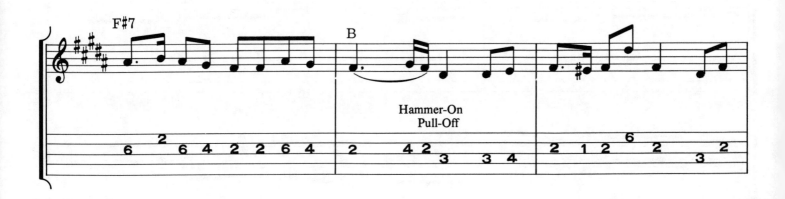

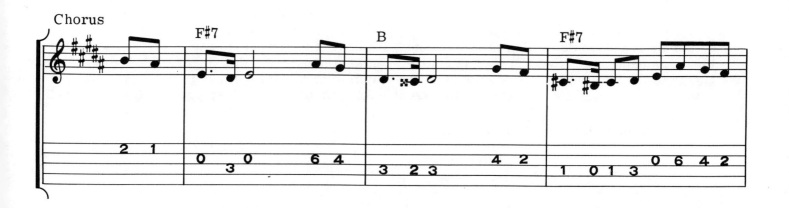

HONESAKALA

This lovely waltz is also in Low G String Tuning. The second part introduces a technique known as delayed picking   This can be done by using thumb and index finger. The index finger leads with the top melody note and the thumb follows with the lower harmony note. This is a common Hawaiian steel guitar technique, with a nice touch of syncopation.

"Honesakala" means honeysuckle.

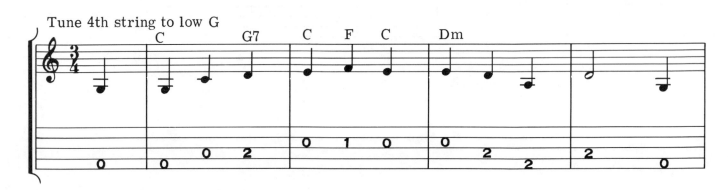

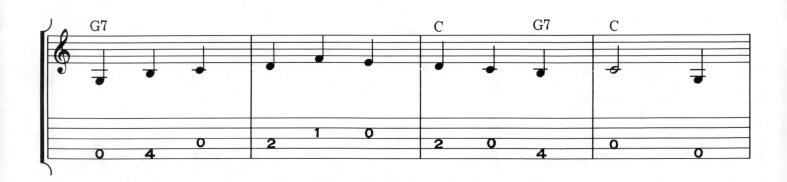

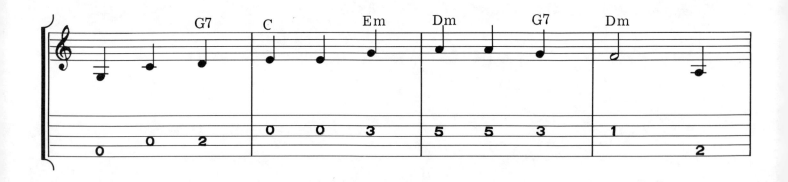

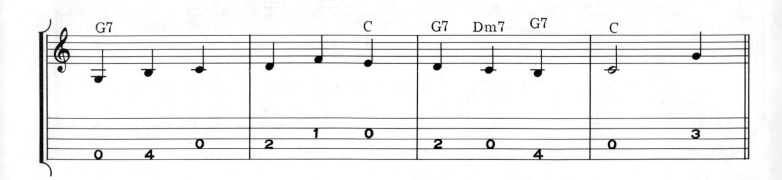

MAUI NO KA O

You may recognize this melody. It is the original of several modern variants. They go by the names "Steel Guitar Chimes" and "Dobro Chimes", but this is the one that started it all! The second part features the delayed picking technique.

Tune 4th string to low G

LILIU E

Liliu E is one song that can be played successfully in either low or high G tuning. It can be done best using four-finger picking. On held chords, the picking pattern is: 1st string, 4th string, 2 middle strings, 4th string. It was written for Queen Liliuokalani and is known as the "Queen's Hula".

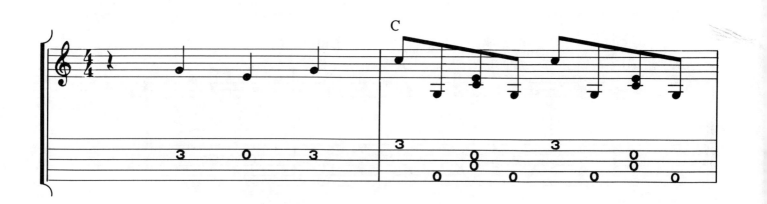

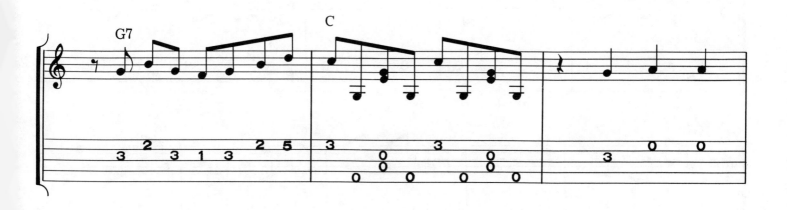

WALTZ FOR MY DEAR

This sweet love song makes good use of left hand chord positions. Thumb and index finger picking works well on this waltz, which is set off nicely by the light sound of the ukulele.

KUWILI

This old Hawaiian Hula song should be played at a moderate pace. See if you can come up with variations of your own, as is done with "Hame Pila" and "Hiilawe" in this book. This can also be done "duelling" style, joining together at the vamp.

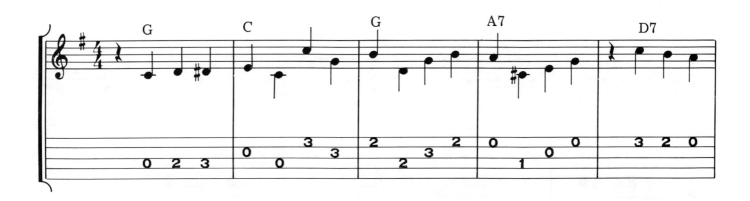

KUU IPO I KA HEE PUE ONE

The word Ipo means Sweetheart in Hawaiian. This is a fingerpicking tune and can be done in four-finger or two-finger style. Play it in a gently flowing fashion, with your sweetheart in mind.

Tune 4th string to low G

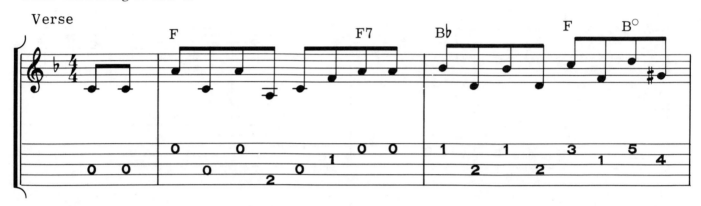

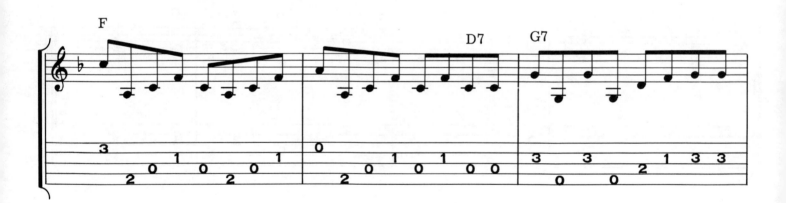

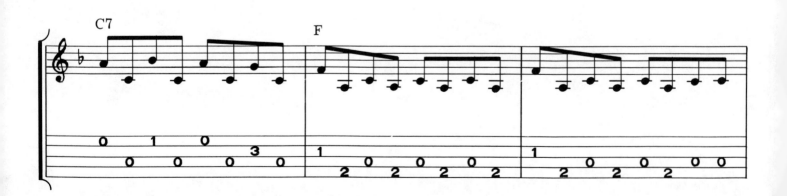

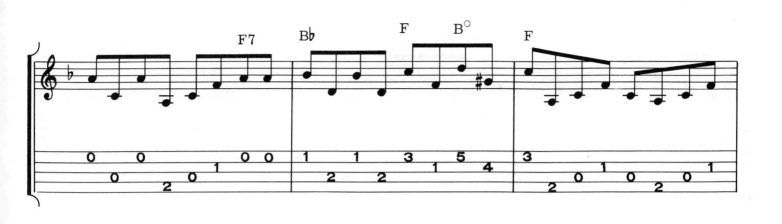
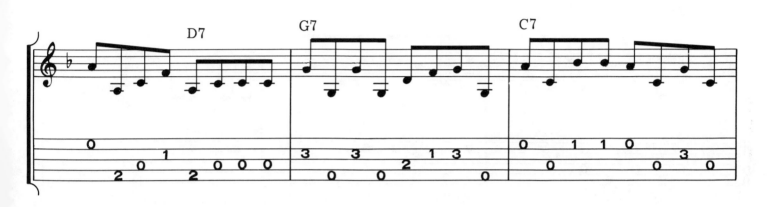
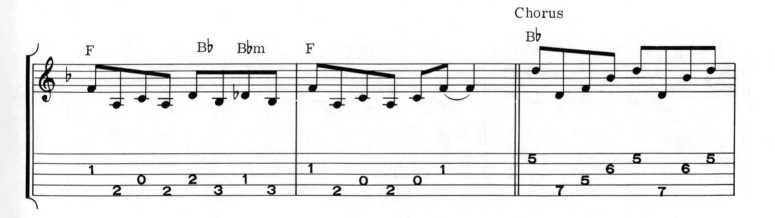

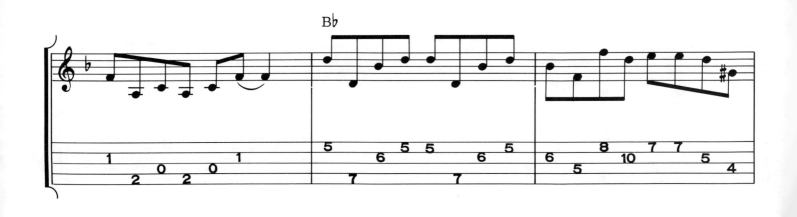

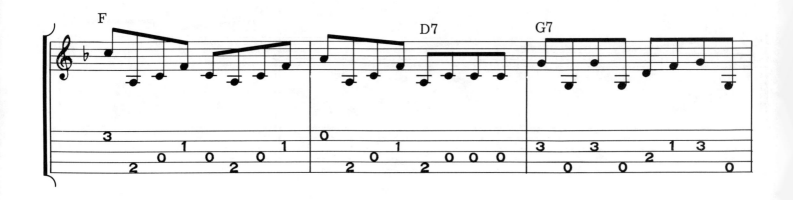

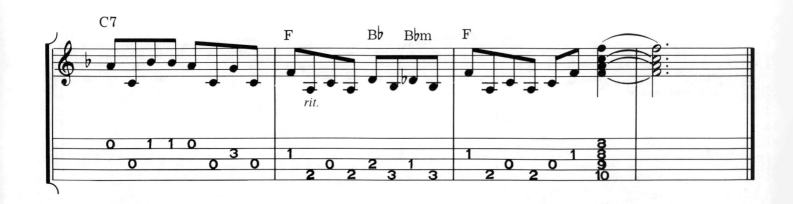

PAAHANA

This ancient melody is reflected in many more modern compositions. Pay particular attention to the sound of the transitional phrase in the last bar.

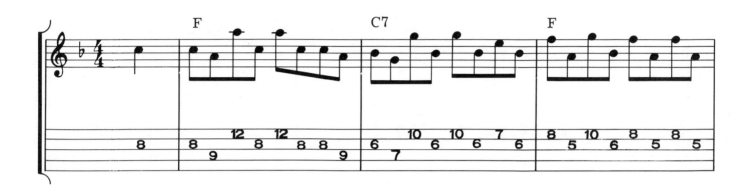

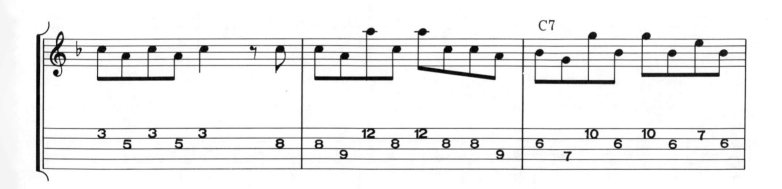

THIS PRETTY UKULELE

A bouncy ditty captures the spirit which lead many to translate Ukulele as "Jumping Flea". It could also be translated as "The gift that came", indicating the gift Hawaii received from Portugal.

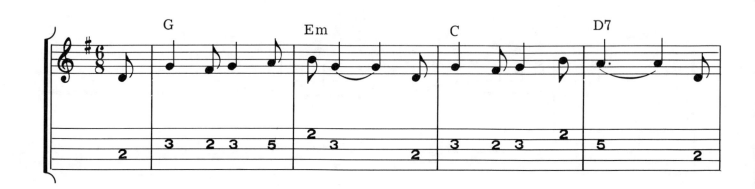

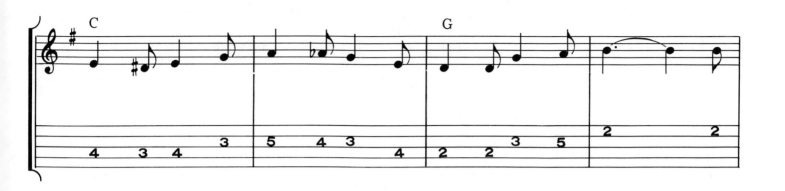

MAUNA KEA

MAUNA KEA is the mountain on the big island of Hawaii. It is snowpeaked for nine months of the year. The name means "white mountain". The song can be done with a two-finger pattern, using thumb and index finger. Figuring the chord positions for the D, E7, and A7 before you start will simplify playing the song.

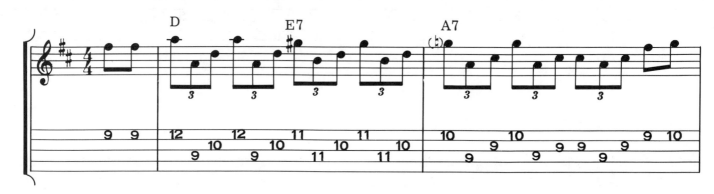

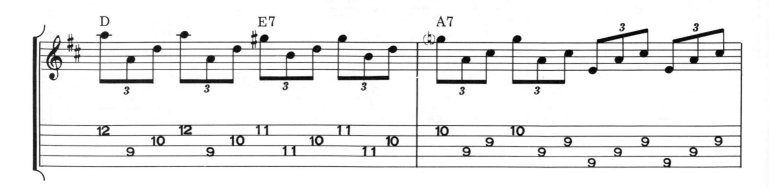

44

LEI NANI

Another closed position tune, "Lei Nani" means "beautiful lei". Play it at a moderate tempo.

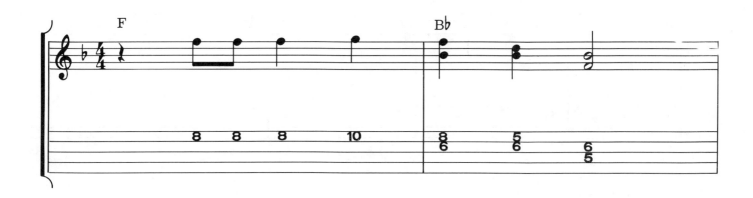

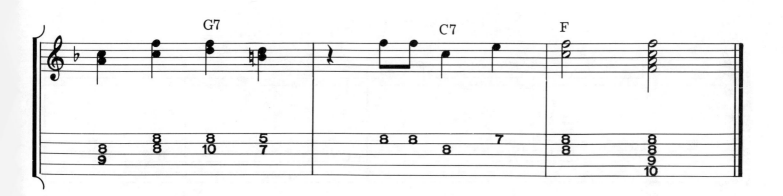

SWEET LEI MAMO

This song was among those recorded by the Ellis Brothers and Madame Alapai in one of the first Victor recording sessions. It also is in a closed position.

Verse

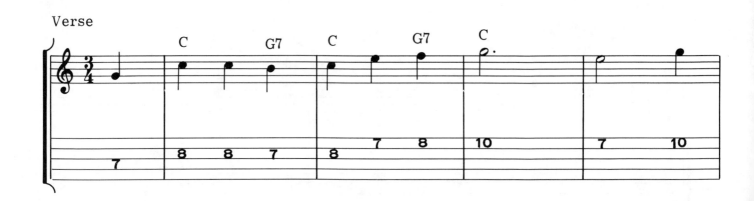

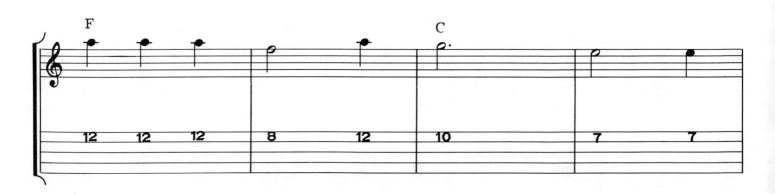

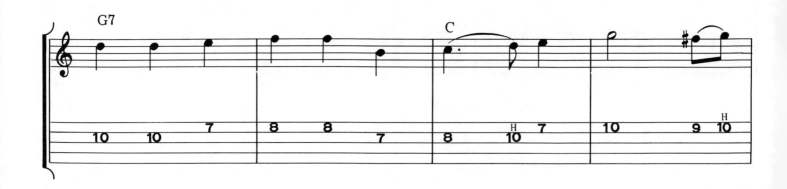

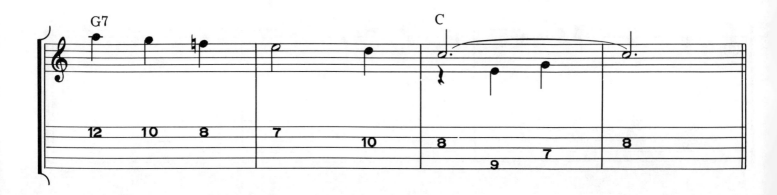

Chorus

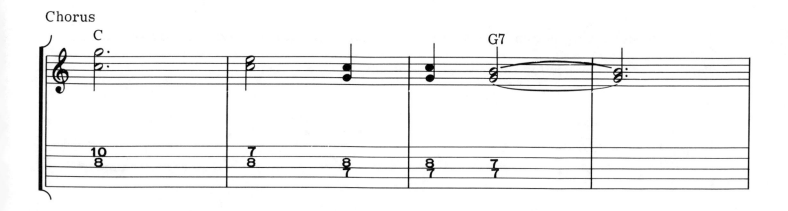

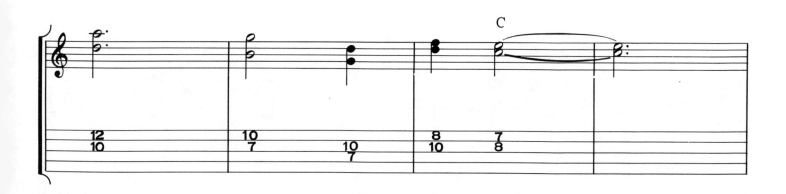

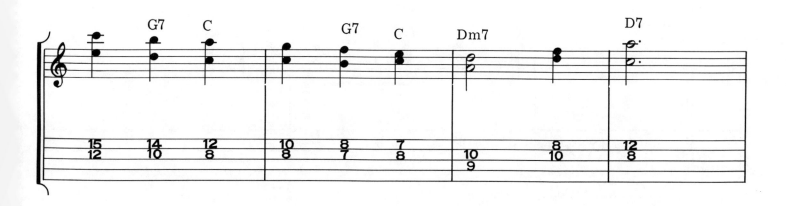

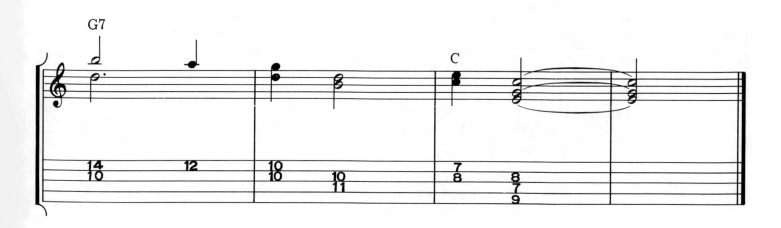

HULA FOR KEN

A modern composition in an ancient style, this tune can be played as fast as you are able. It is a thank you for the musical generosity of Ken Eidson.

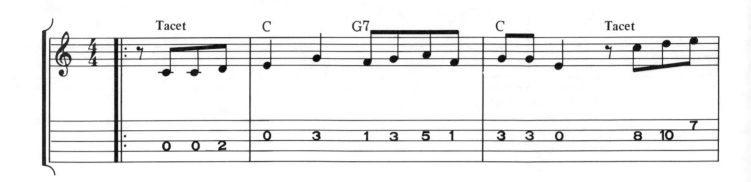

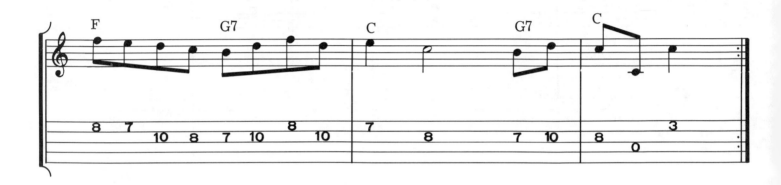

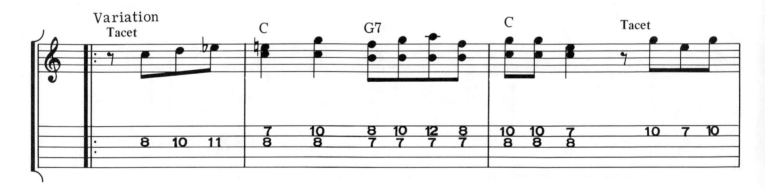

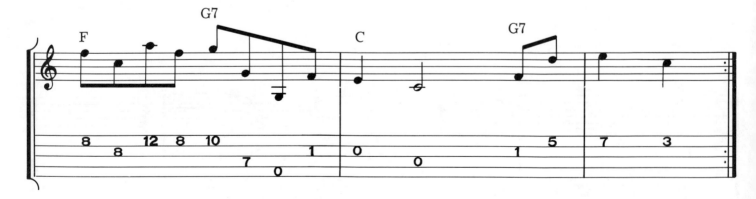

UA LIKE NO A LIKE

Also known as "Sweet Constancy" or "My Heart's Choice". This song has been a favorite for a century. Parallel thirds are used throughout the arrangement. The left hand fingering patterns used are worth noting, as they can provide a fairly easy way to harmonize songs.

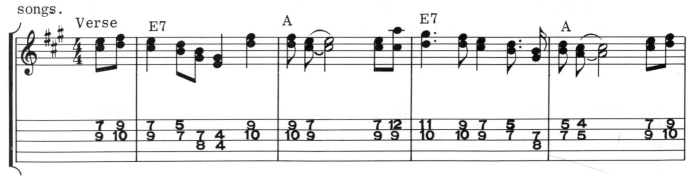

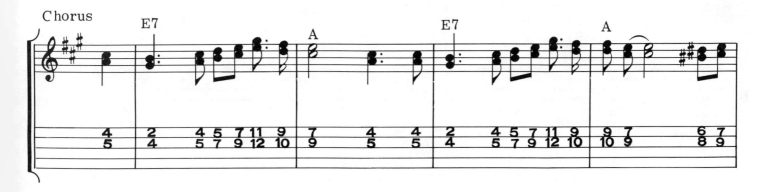

LEI OHU

This song can be played mostly out of the G chord with the barre at the seventh fret:

This simple song shows how strongly a Hawaiian feel can be gained by using intervals of the sixth. Singers would typically break into falsetto as they reach the sixth from below. Watch for this in other songs.

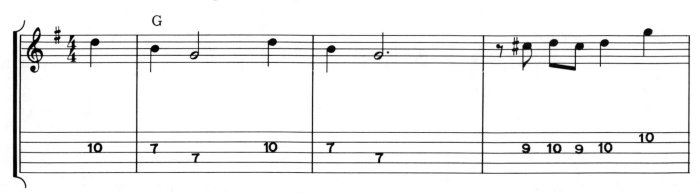

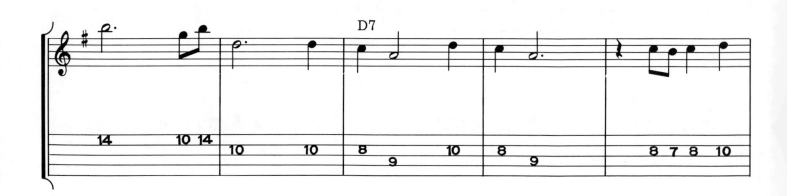

THINK PALM TREES

Practice with three string chords and left hand ornaments combined with a nostalgic
air give the perceptive player new musical insights along old familiar paths.

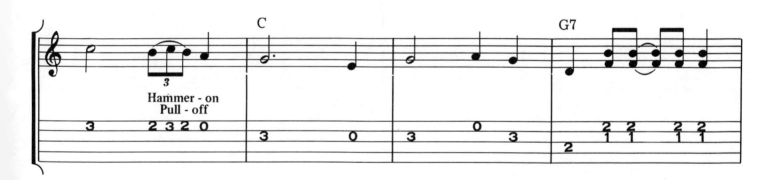

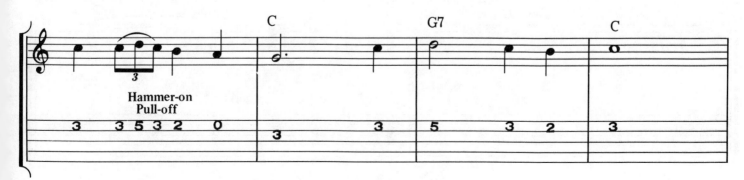

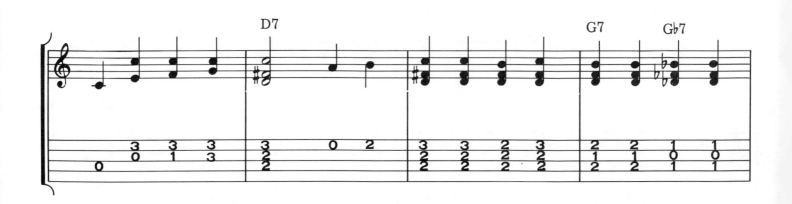

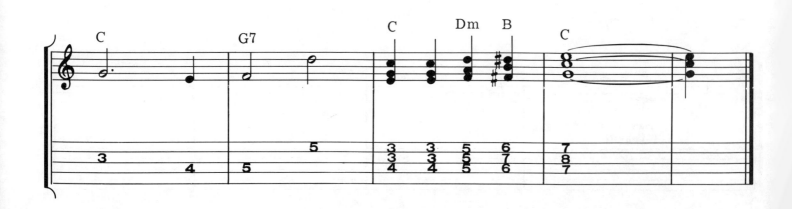

HAWAII PONOI

This is the State Song. It should be played like a stately march. It was based on "God Save the King".

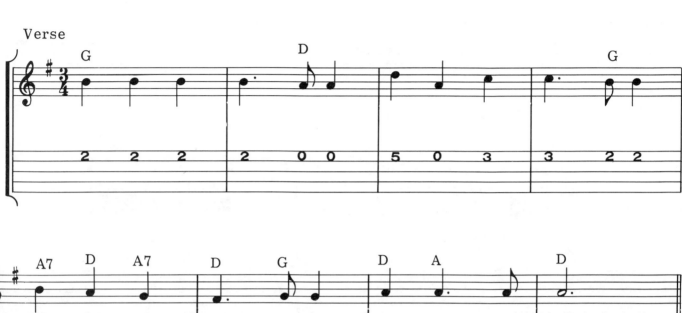

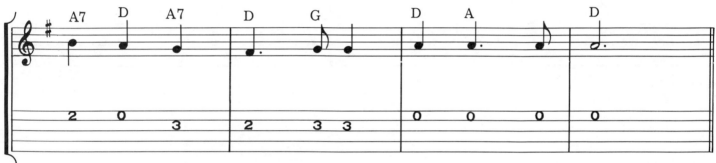

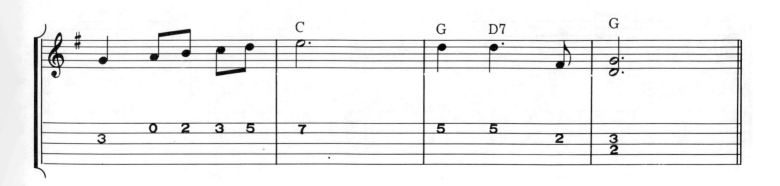

Var.1
Verse

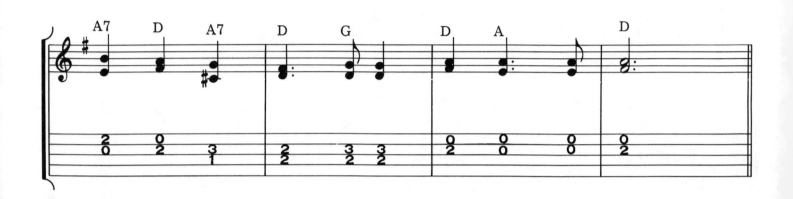

Chorus

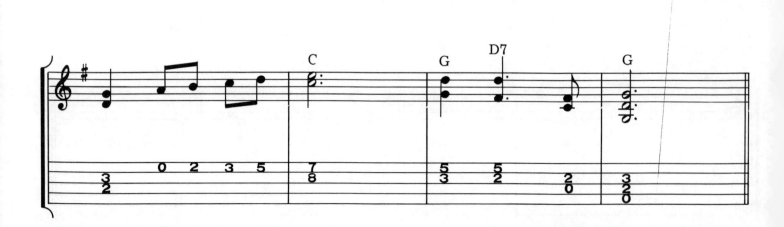

Var.2

Verse

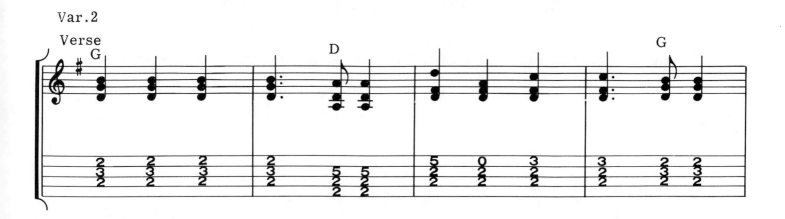

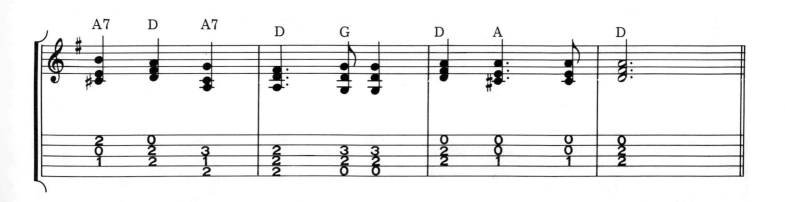

Chorus

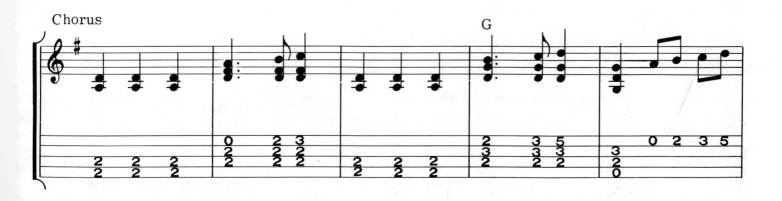

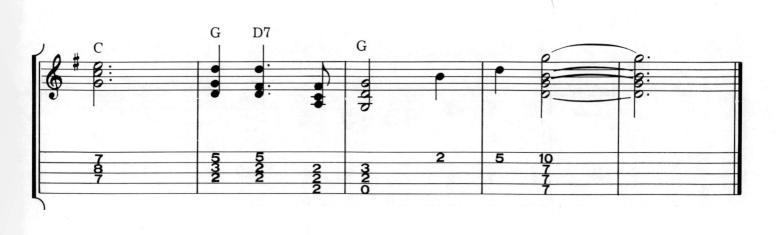

55

ALOHA NO WAU I KO MAKA

This is a good exercise in tremolo. Notes longer than the quarter note should be played with tremolo. This song is based on the folk music of early settlers in Hawaii.

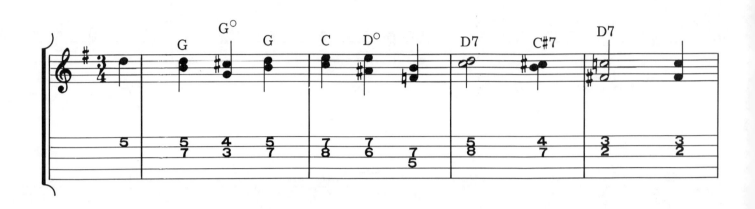

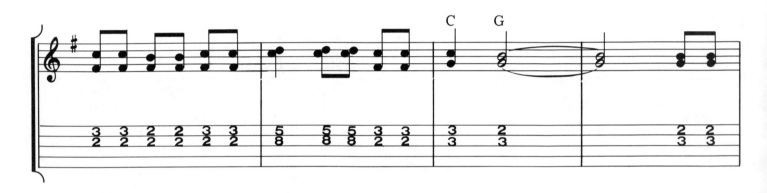

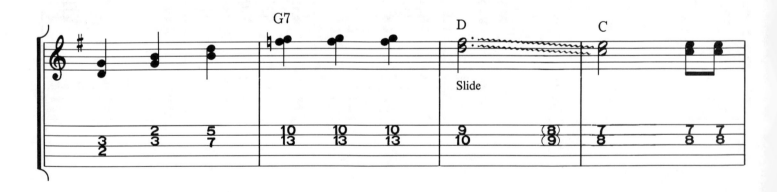

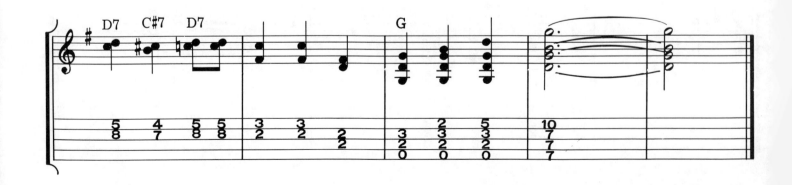

HAME PILA

This song can be done as a duet in a "duelling" style, if you want to try it with a friend. The eighth note rests show when to switch parts - Don't forget to strum chords when your partner solos. Try some upper position chords for the first two versions for a special sound. Play it fast.

HALONA

"Halona" is another of the many beautiful waltzes in Hawaiian music. Play it with a

lilt and liberal use of tremolo. It is one of the few Hawaiian songs to bear a Spanish

influence.

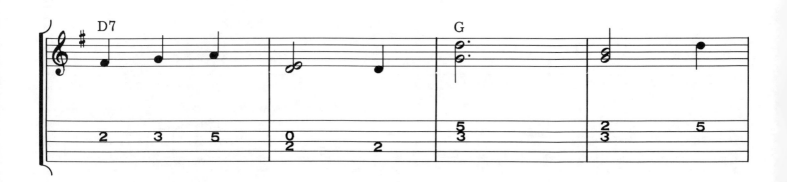

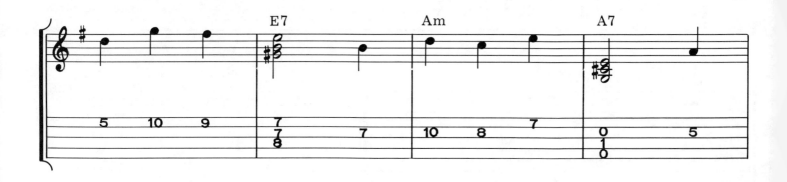

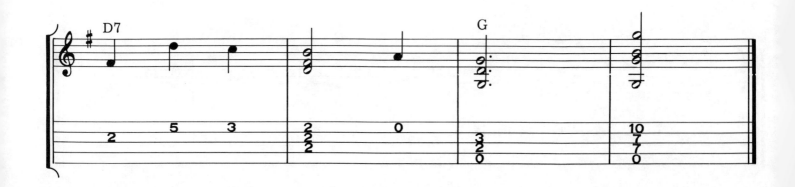

HIILAWE

Hiilawe is a set of waterfalls on the big island of Hawaii. The song itself is of ancient origin. It is probably the most recorded of the old Hawaiian songs. It should be played very fast. Hiilawe is great fun played dueling style.

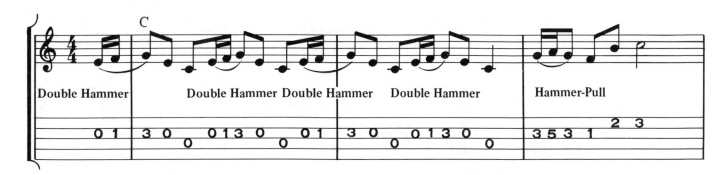

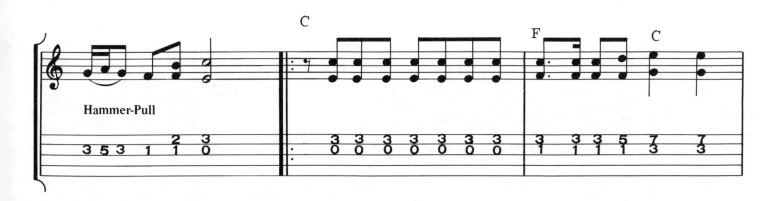

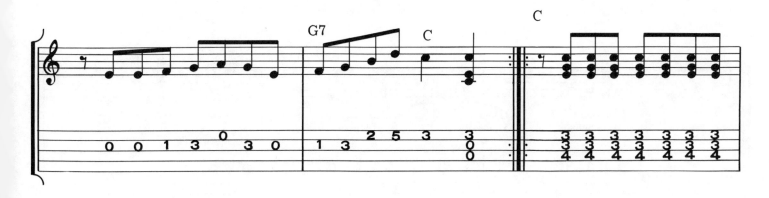

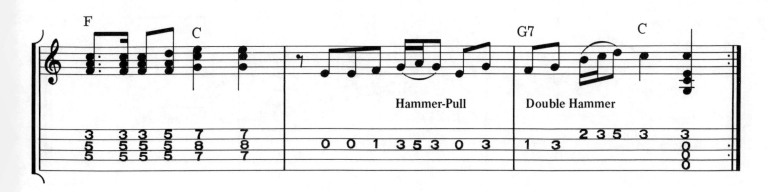

HEEIA

This is a name chant or "mele inoa" for King Kalakaua. It is a favorite slack key guitar number. Use the Molokai Strum with it.

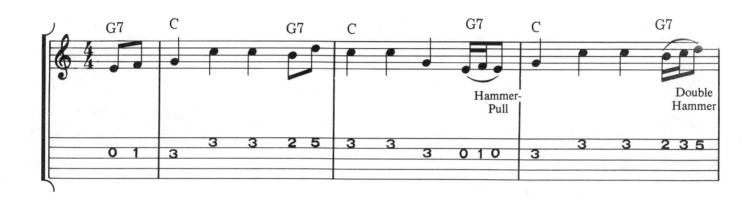

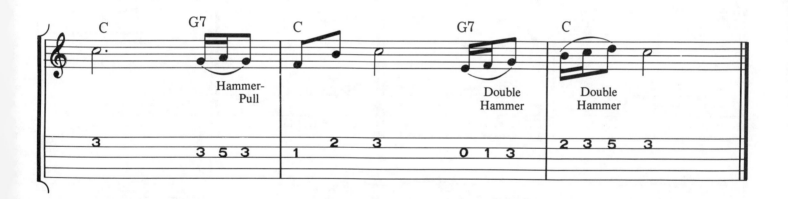

BETSY'S TUNE OR ELIKAPEKA

This tune has many typical ornaments and frills used in Hawaiian slack key music.
Play it as fast as you are able. Try slipping some of these ornaments into your playing
on other songs. Your left hand will get a real work out.

SWEET LEI LEHUA

Lehua is the flower of the big island of Hawaii. It looks like a big red puff-ball. If you pick one, the sky is supposed to rain.

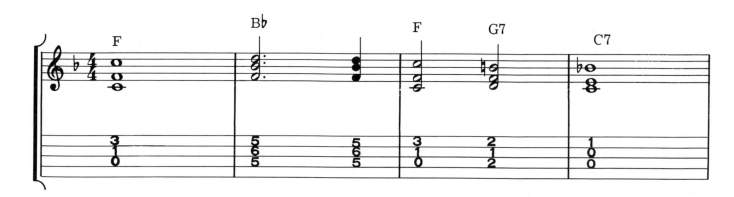

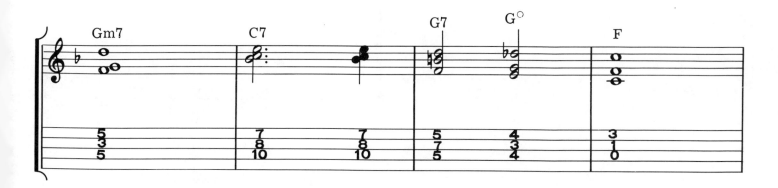

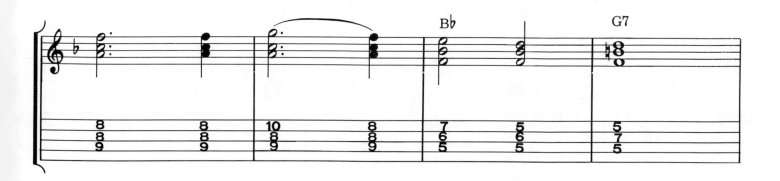

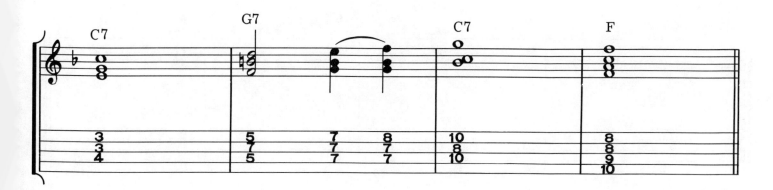

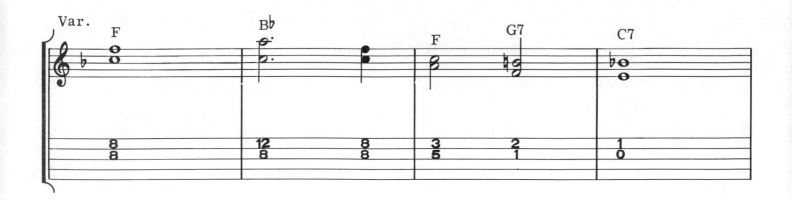
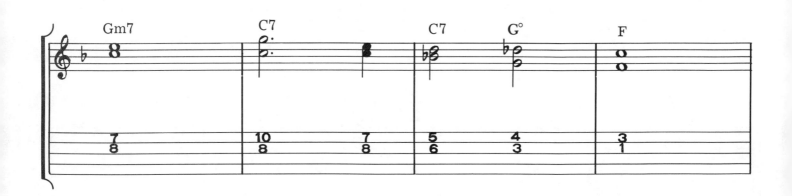
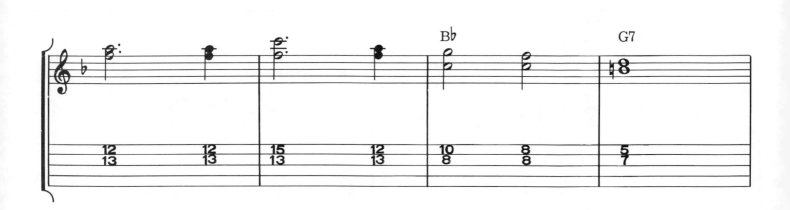
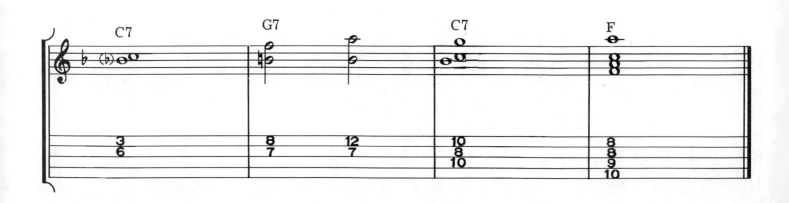

MANU OO

"Manu Oo" features three string chords on longer notes. Try tremolo on these chords. Then try tremolo on all the notes and see what you prefer. Do not play it too fast, but try to inject feeling into a leisurely rendition.

HANOHANO HANALEI

Beautiful Hanalei valley is on the island of Kauai. You can play this piece with basic thumb strumming if you want to. It plays easily with no extra fingers unless you want to use them!

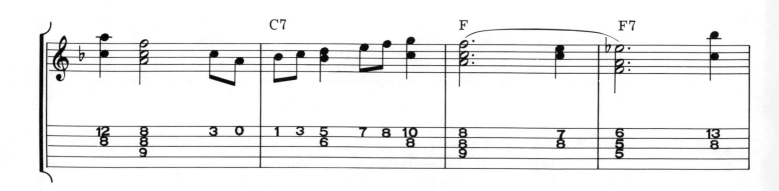

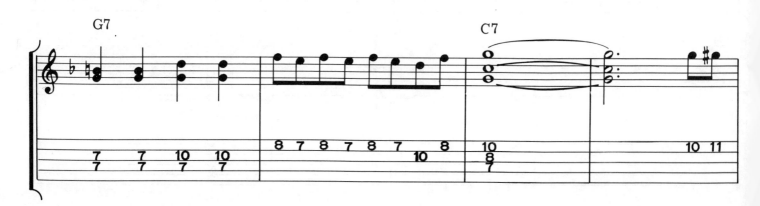

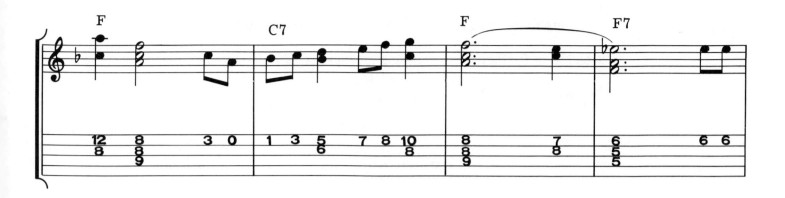

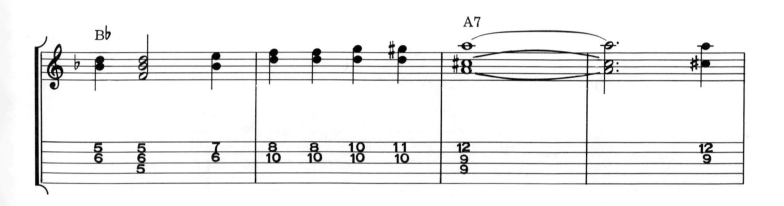

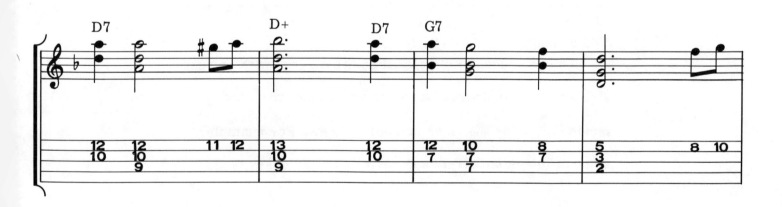

LEI OHAOHA

This song is arranged in the rather unlikely key of G-flat in order to further your working knowledge of playing from the barre position.

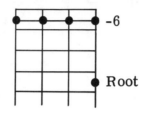

"Playing in position" gives us a major scale like this:

This is a completely closed position song, with no open strings. Such songs can be moved up or down the neck by moving all notes the same number of frets. For example, move all notes up 1 fret, and you will be in the key of G.

LEI OHAOHA

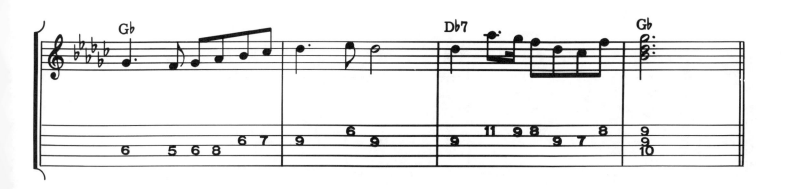

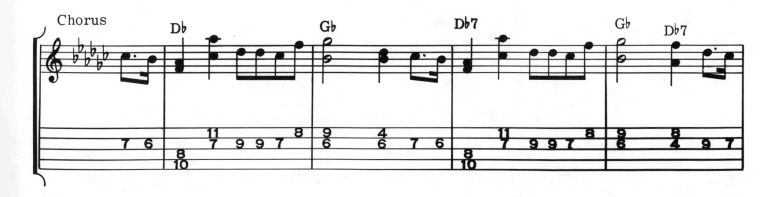

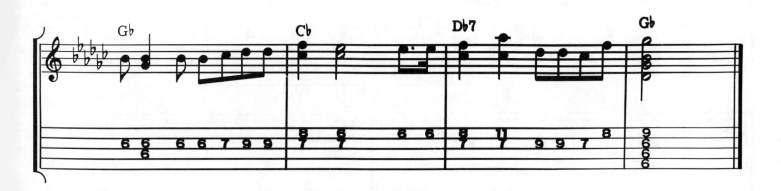

PULUPE NEI ILI I KE ANU

This waltz, also known as "Beautiful Lanihuli", features runs across the chords on the held notes. These can be played with the thumb or using four fingers, being sure to let the top note of the chord ring throughout the run.

NUUANU WAIPUNA

This song will give additional practice with three string chords. It is in closed position.

Try moving it down the neck one fret at a time and see how the tone quality changes.

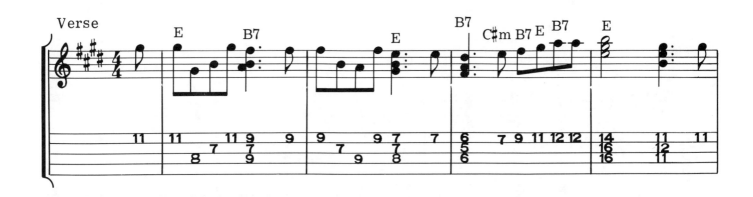

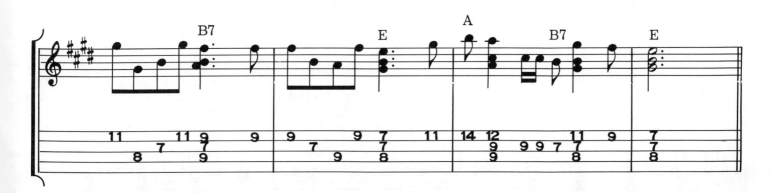

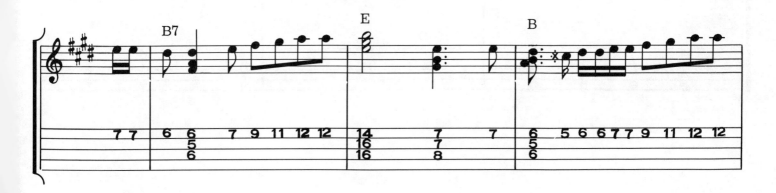

HULA O MAKEE

This song **was one of the earliest** to be recorded by William Kualii Ellis and his brother John **Kapilikea Ellis on Victor records. Our** arrangement features four string chords for a rich, **full sound.**

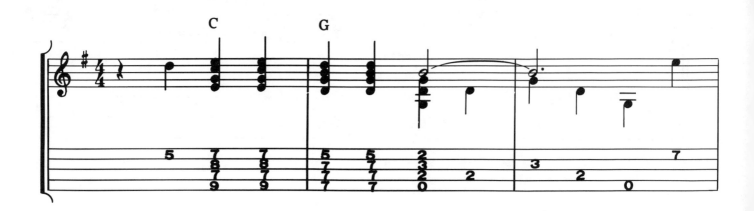

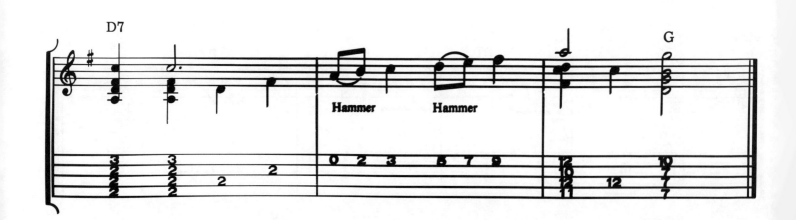

ALOHA OE

The word "Aloha" means "love" more than simply "hello" or goodbye". This is one of many famous Hawaiian songs written by royalty. "Aloha Oe" was written by Queen Lilio-kulani. It was written as a love song, not a farewell long, and is undoubtably Hawaii's best known song. Play it slowly, with tremolo.

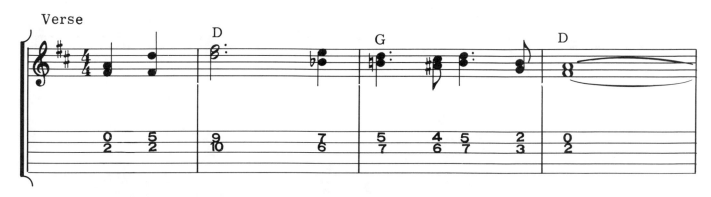

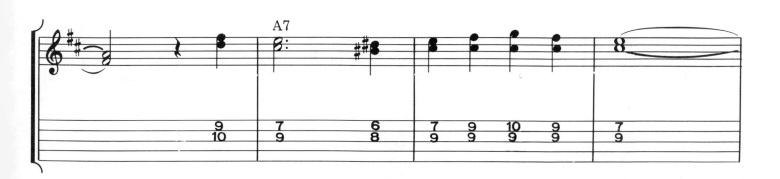

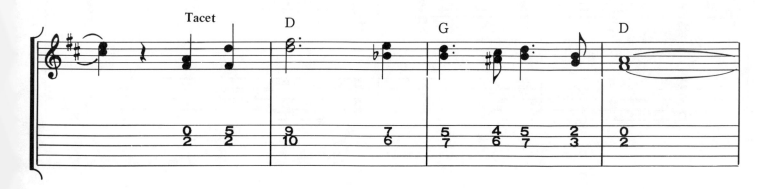

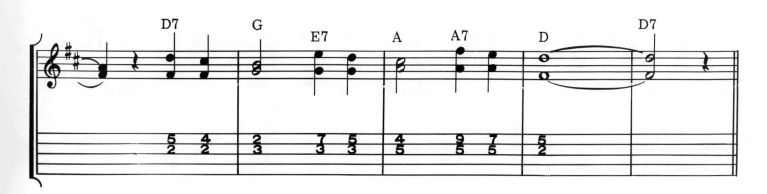

Refrain

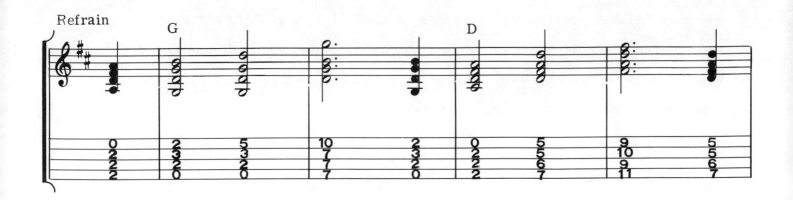

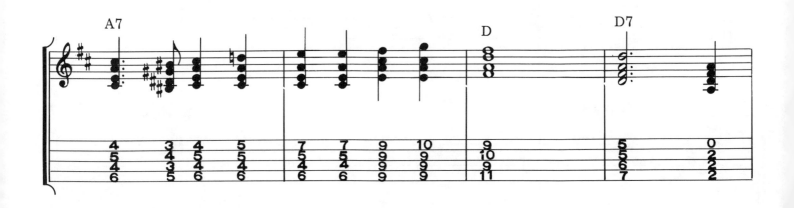

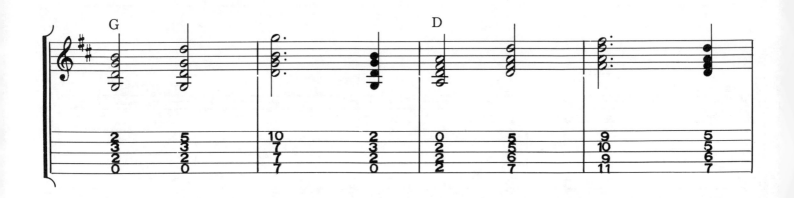

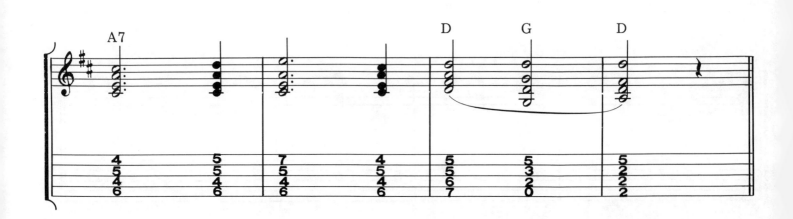

Refrain var.

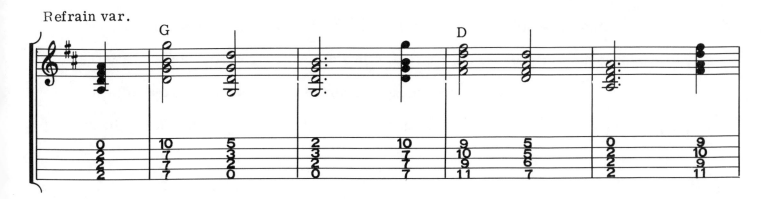

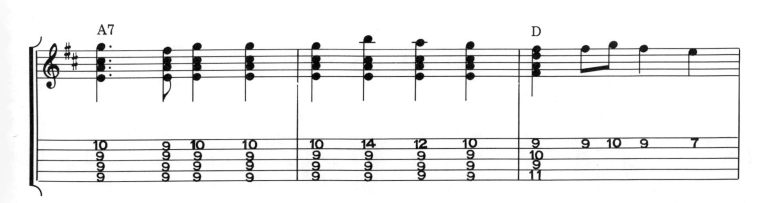

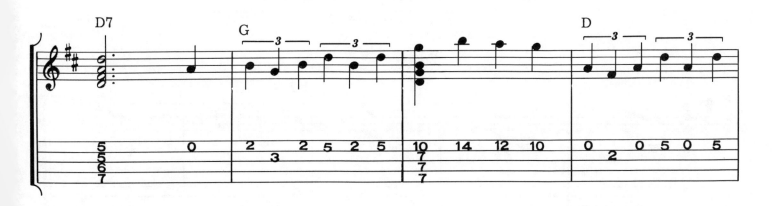

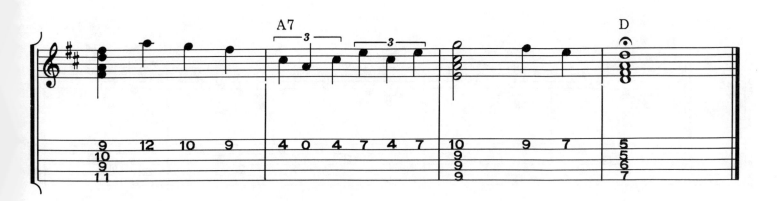

FRIEND'S LULLABY

This song should be picked with all four fingers on the right hand. Each finger gets its own string and never need stray. There are five different right hand picking patterns. Start the song slowly. There is no need for speed, and the more difficult latter patterns will appreciate a leisurely beginning. Serenade your cat to sleep with "Friend's Lullaby"!

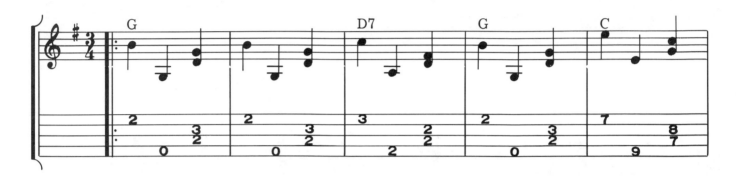

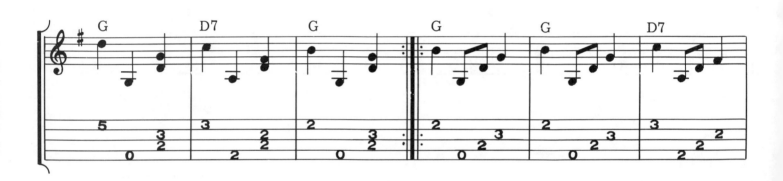

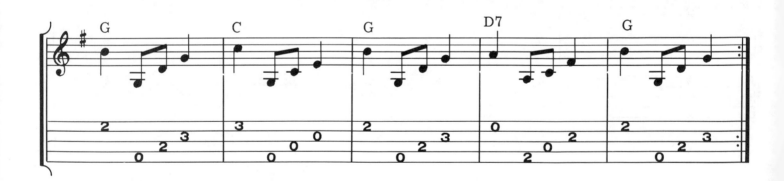

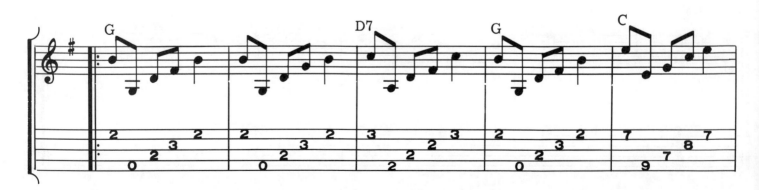

76

WILIWILI WAI

"Wiliwili Wai" was featured on the first radio broadcast beamed at the U.S. mainland.

It is a humorous observation of the first water sprinkler seen in Hawaii.

PUA SADINIA

This is an example of the transitional hula hui songs which bridged the stylistic gap between ancient chants and hulas and the more modern music. The chorus uses the delayed picking technique with a few fill notes on the G string on longer notes. Don't let these fill notes confuse you, since they won't fit into the pattern of the delayed picking technique.

MOANI KE ALA

This song, in the key of E, helps to acquaint you with more closed position playing. After you learn it in the key of E, try it in a higher key by playing the same notes a fret or two higher. There are no open strings in this arrangement, so the whole song is totally movable. It was written by Prince Leleiohoka who in his 23 years contributed some of the prettiest melodies composed by Hawaiian royalty.

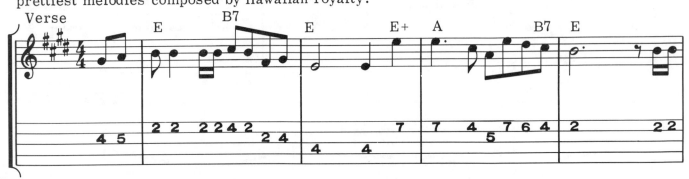

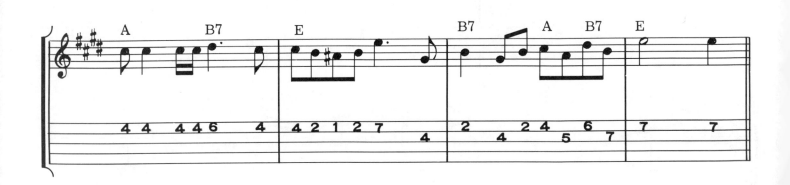

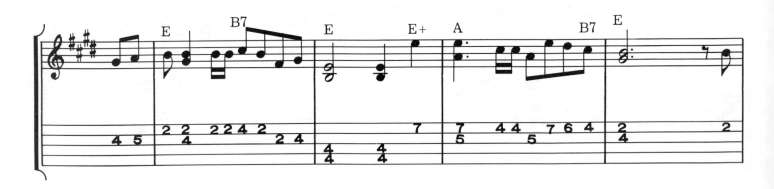

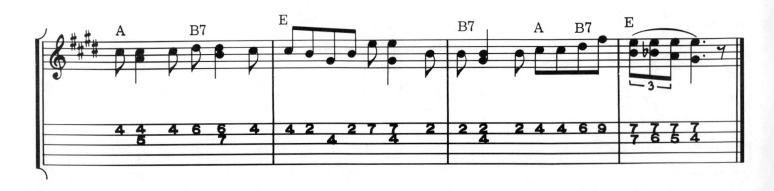

MAKALAPUA-VERSION 1

The use of grace notes in the first half of this arrangement, involving many Hammer-ons and Pull-offs in rapid succession, is in close imitation of the famous "slack key" style of guitar. Play the extra notes carefully because they are very important to the flavor of the music. Play it as a slow ballad. Be sure to bring out the chords in the chorus, either by tremolo or by letting them ring out.

This song was adapted from the hymn "Would I Were With Thee". It was a favorite of Queen Liliokulani, and it was sung as her funeral dirge. Notice the use of parallel thirds in Version 2. We present "Makalapua" in two versions.

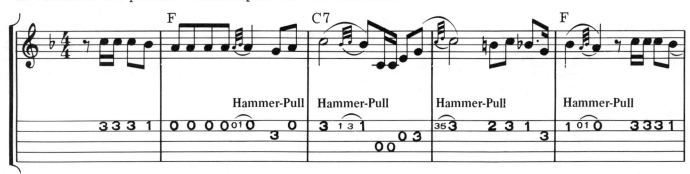

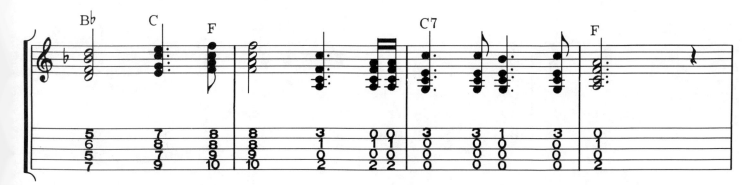

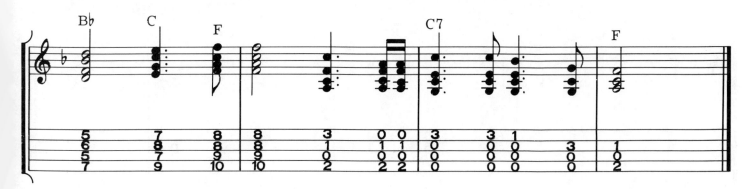

MAKALAPUA—VERSION 2

LUANA'S DANCE

Play this song as fast as you can. It contains a goodly amount of left hand work, which can be applied as embellishments or accents to other songs.

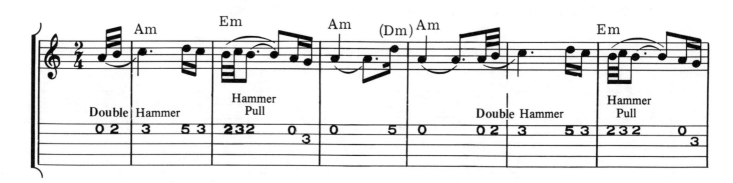

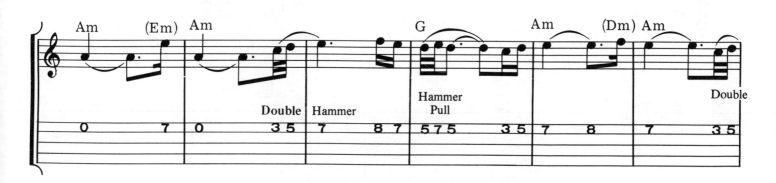

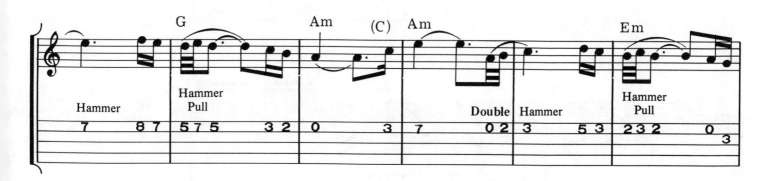

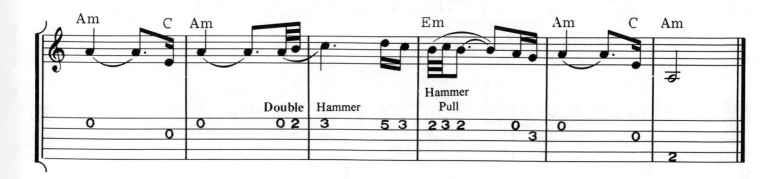

VIOLETA

This song combines many of the techniques we've used earlier. It begins in the G chord position based on a seventh fret barre. It is in closed position throughout, hence is movable. It goes into a passage of delayed picking before returning to G position.

Tune 4th string to low G

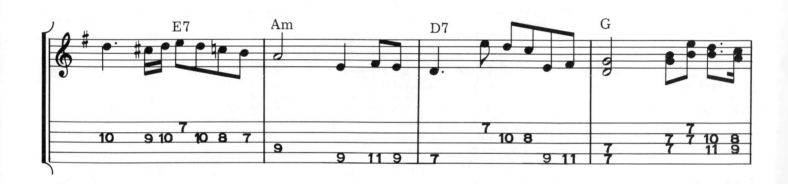

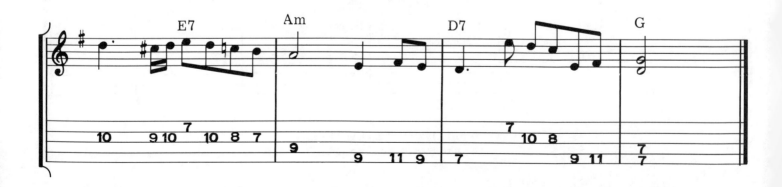

PAUAHI O KALANI

Also known as "Princess Pauahi", the verse of this song is harmonized in sixths,
a common Hawaiian harmony. In the chorus, the harmony becomes more active. Two-finger
picking, with the thumb picking all the lower notes works well.

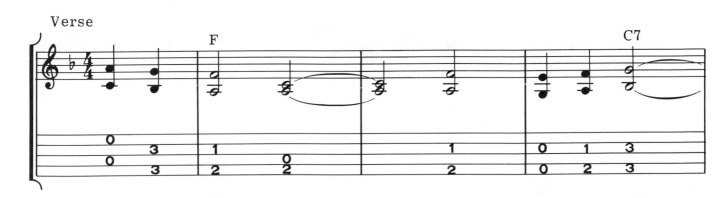

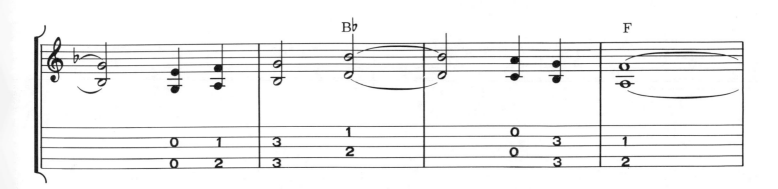

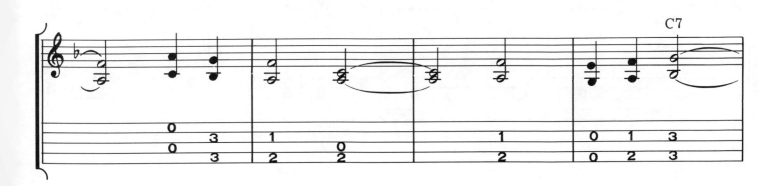

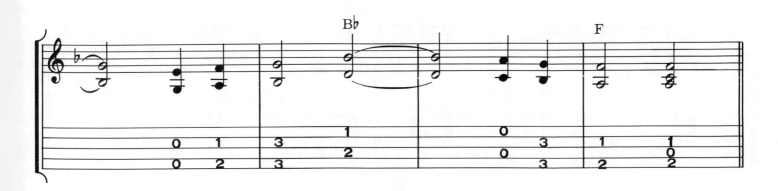

Chorus

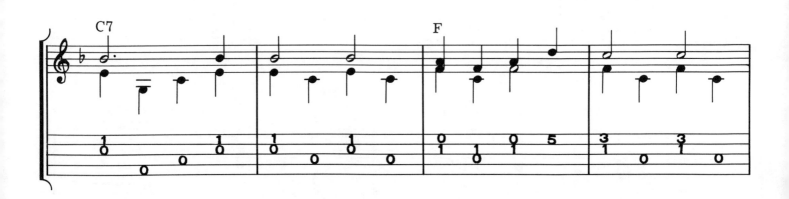

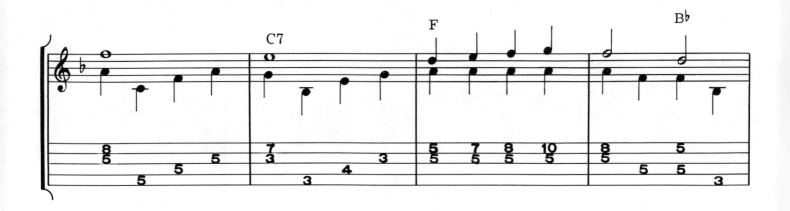

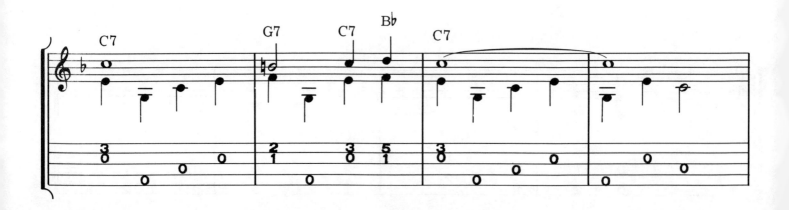

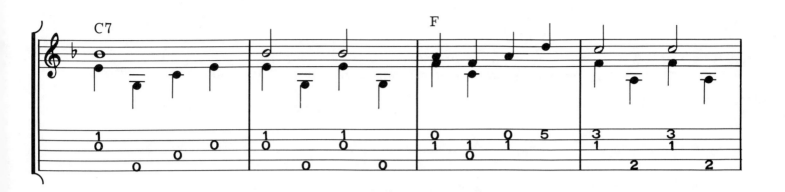

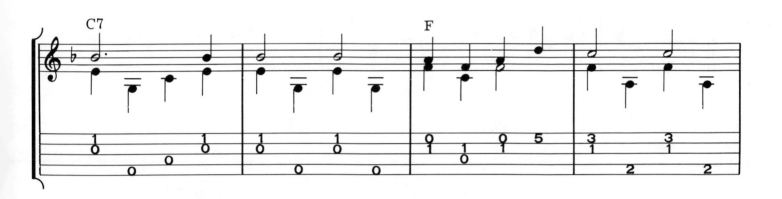

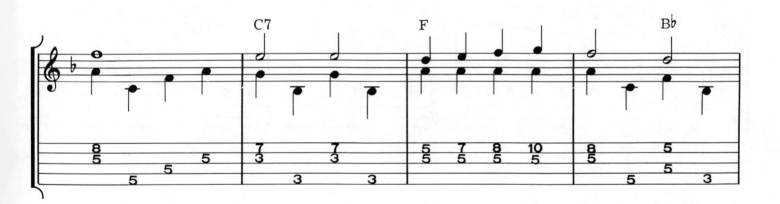

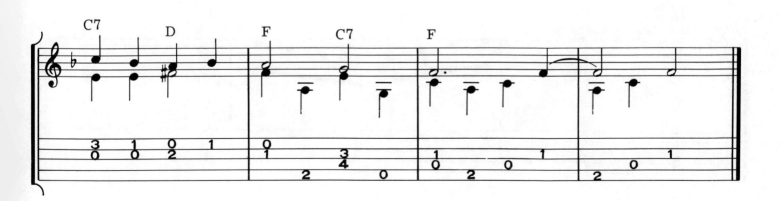

ALEKOKI

This popular traditional song occurs in many versions. It is based on a hula chant.

Play it leisurely. The last two measures can be repeated as a "turnaround".

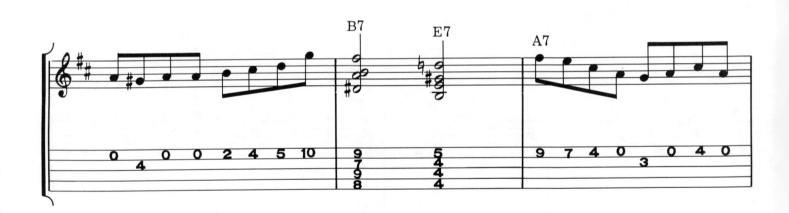

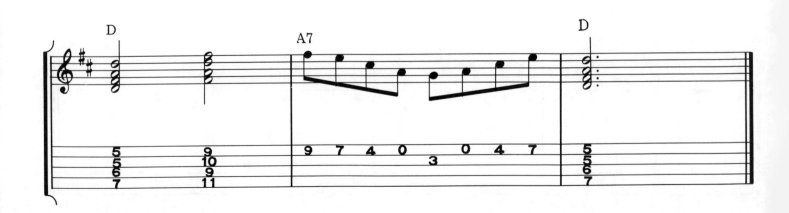

ALIKA

The "Alaska Hula", Alika uses four string chords. Play it at a gentle pace with tremolo on all the half and whole notes.

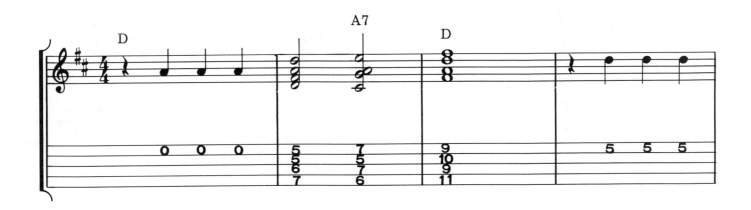

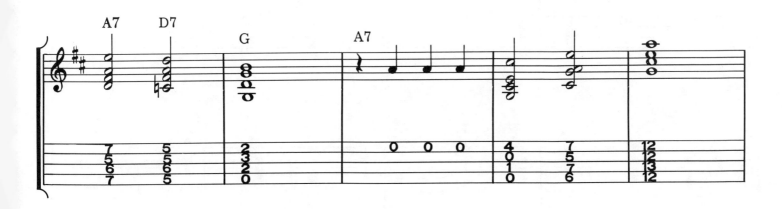

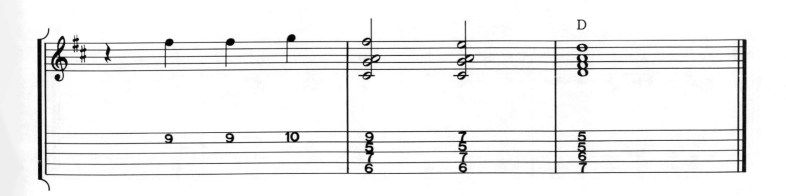

WAIALAE

This waltz is four string chords all the way. Play it at a moderate tempo and let the chords ring.

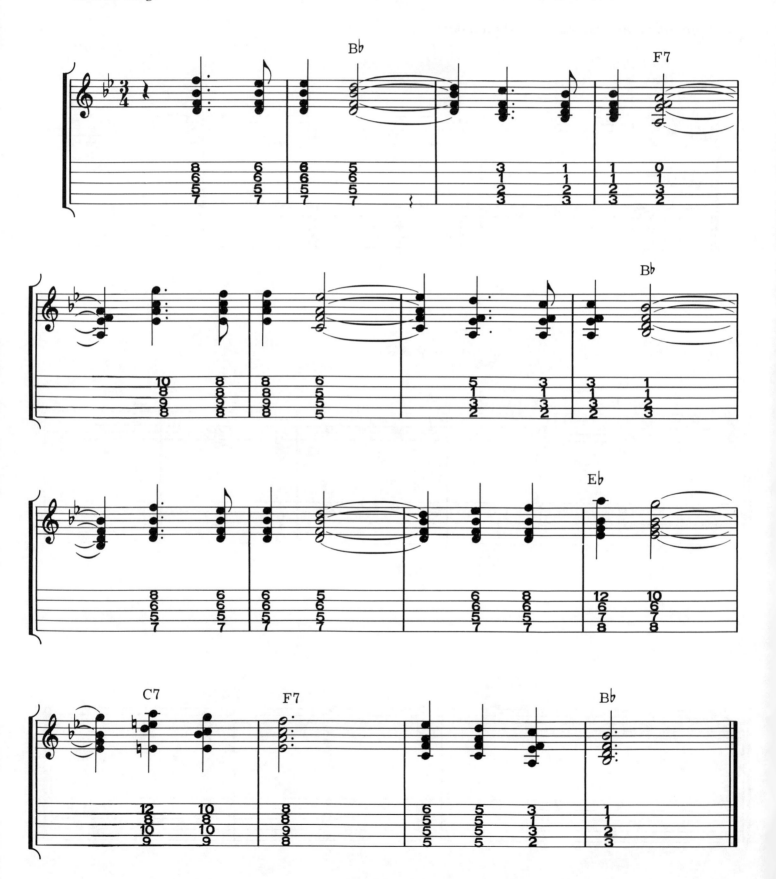

AKAHI HOI

"Tis For Thee Alone", as this song is also called, is arranged in four string chords. Note that the song uses two C chord positions, two Dm chord positions, two G7 chord positions, and one F chord position. These chord positions up and down the neck make this kind of arrangement possible. The more high position chords you know, the easier this gets. Play it at a moderate tempo.

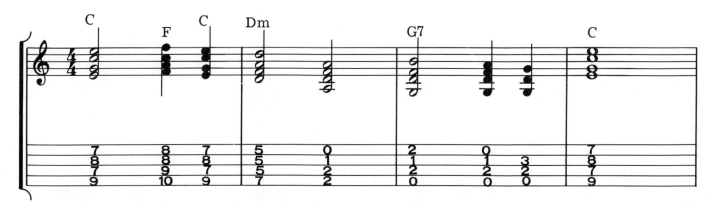

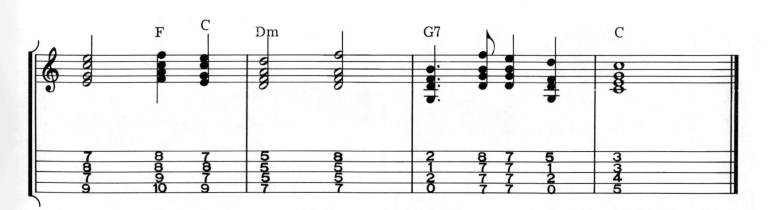

LEI PONI MOI

"Lei Poni Moi", or "Carnation Lei" gives the left hand a work out with its many four string chords up and down the neck. It should be played slowly and expressively.

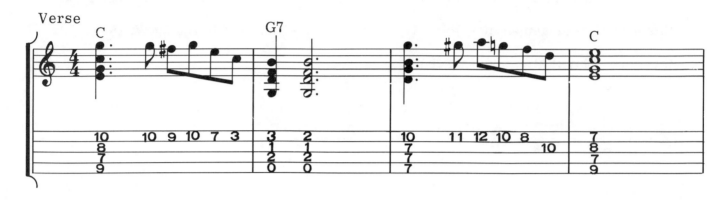

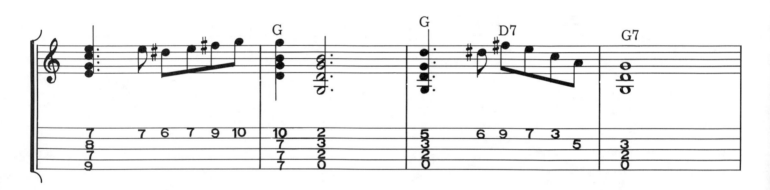

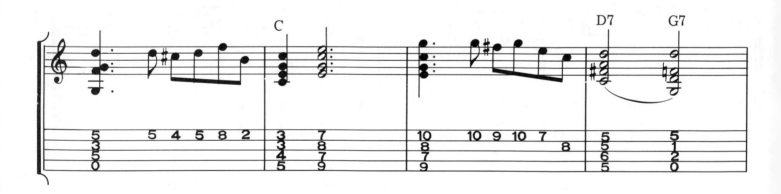

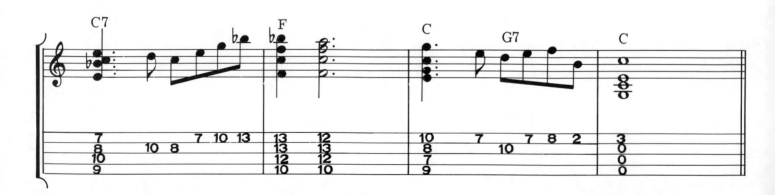

Chorus

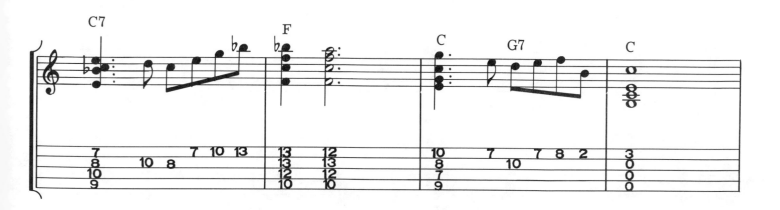

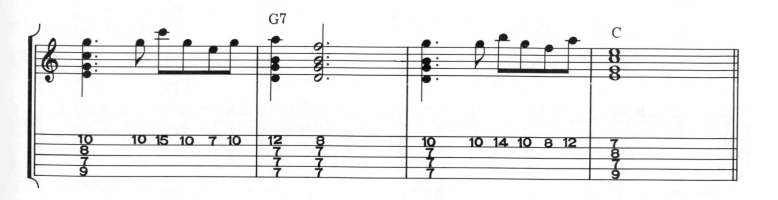

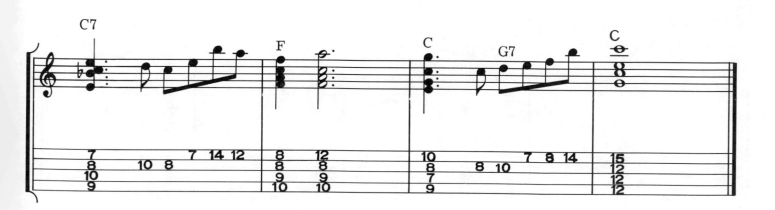

SAKURA

The Portuguese were not the only people to immigrate to Hawaii in the large numbers. The need to find workers for the sugar fields brought settlers from East and West, making Hawaii the cosmopolitan multi-cultured place that it now is. In honor of the Americans of Asian ancestry in Hawaii, we offer a traditional Japanese folk song, "Sakura" or "Cherry Blossoms", arranged for three and four string chords.

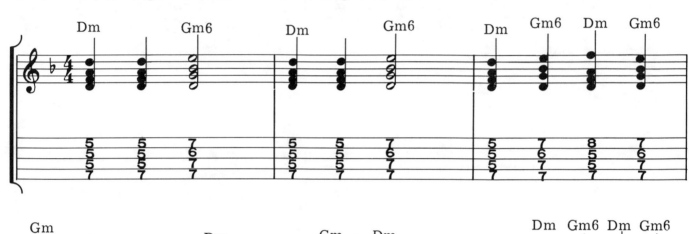

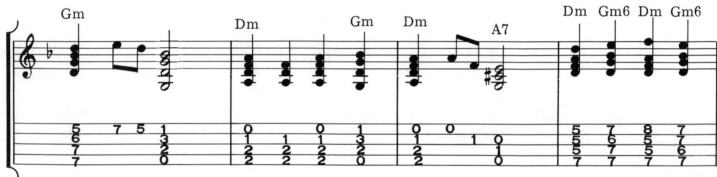

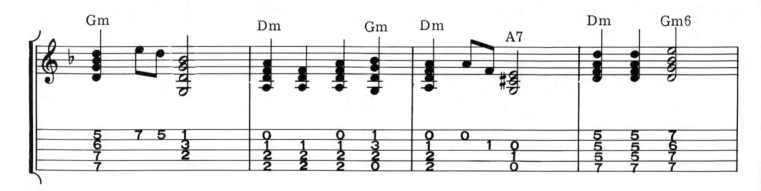

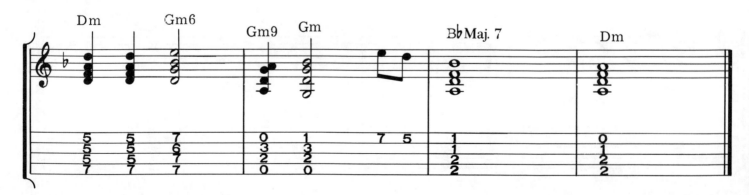

ADVANCED CHORDS

Here are over 300 chords for the ukulele that you may find helpful in your playing. There are many more chords possible, and the more you can play, the more variety you will have. Enjoy.

C

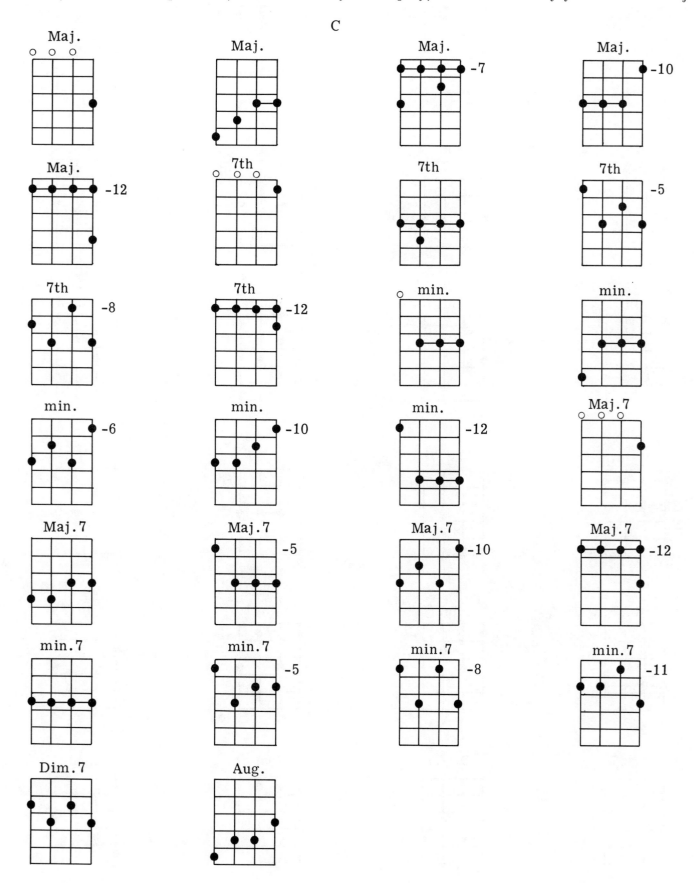

Db / C#

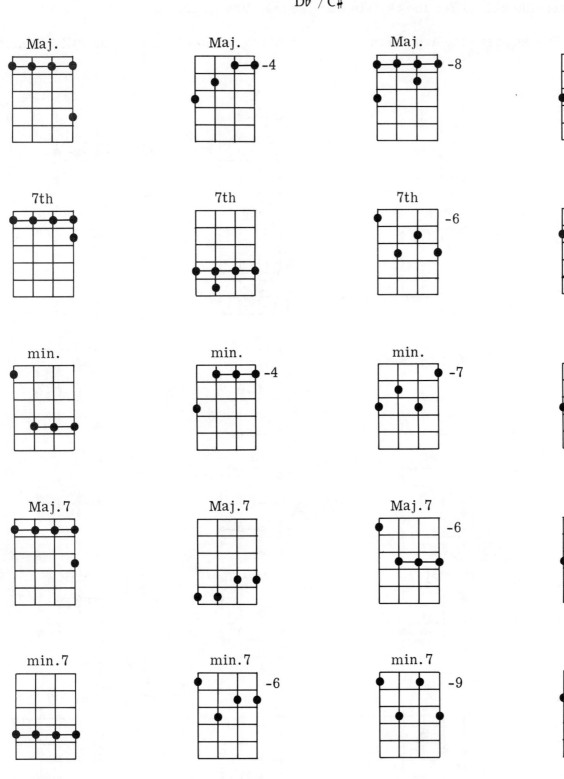

D

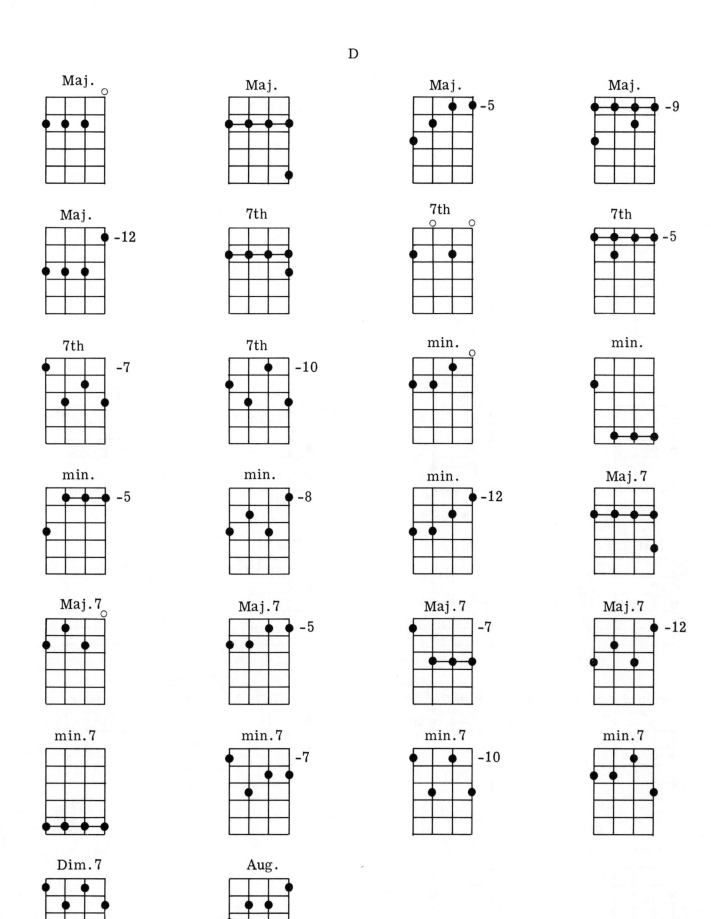

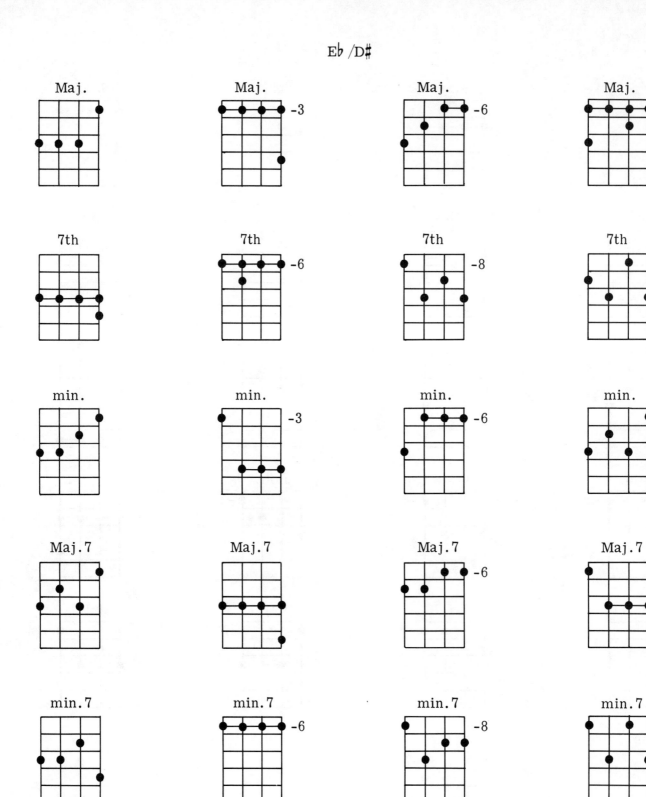

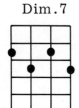

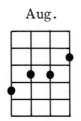

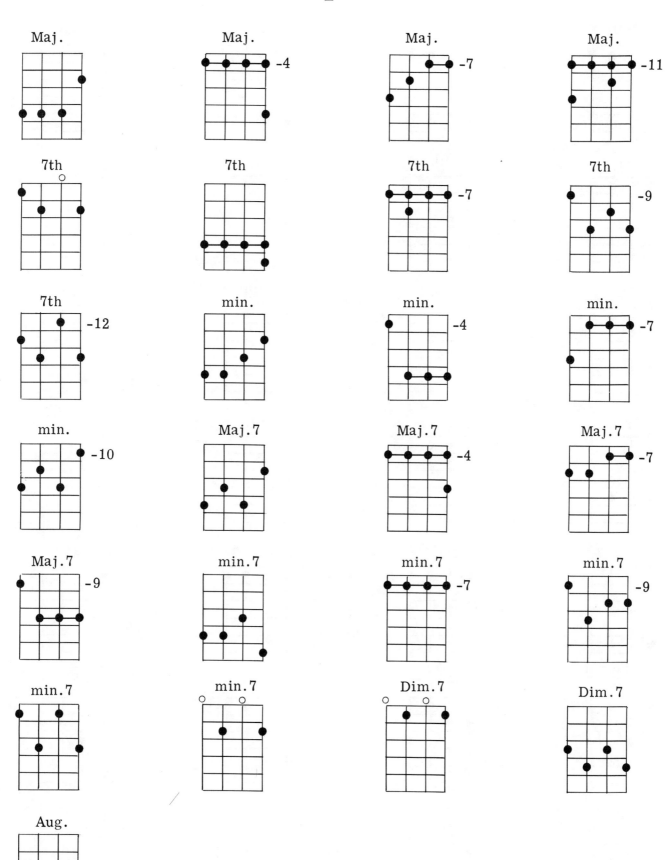

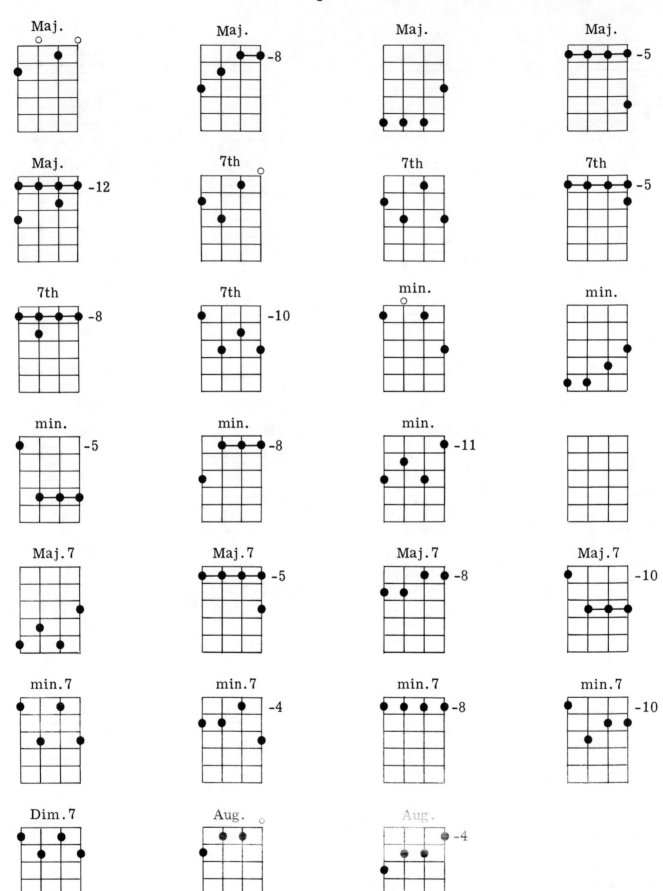

Maj.
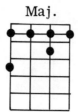

Maj.
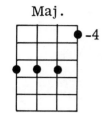
-4

Maj.
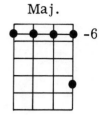
-6

Maj.
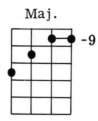
-9

7th
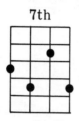

7th
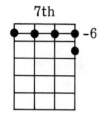
-6

7th
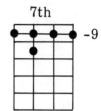
-9

7th
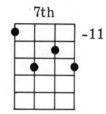
-11

min.
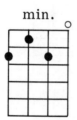

min.
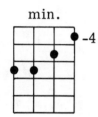
-4

min.
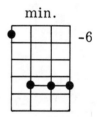
-6

min.
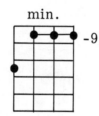
-9

min.
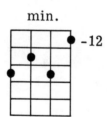
-12

Maj.7
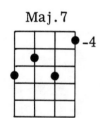
-4

Maj.7
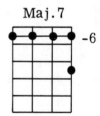
-6

Maj.7
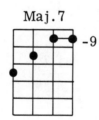
-9

Maj.7
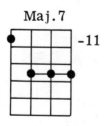
-11

min.7
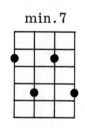

min.7
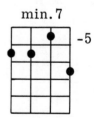
-5

min.7
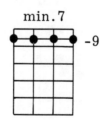
-9

min.7
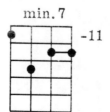
-11

Dim.7

Aug.
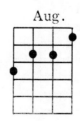

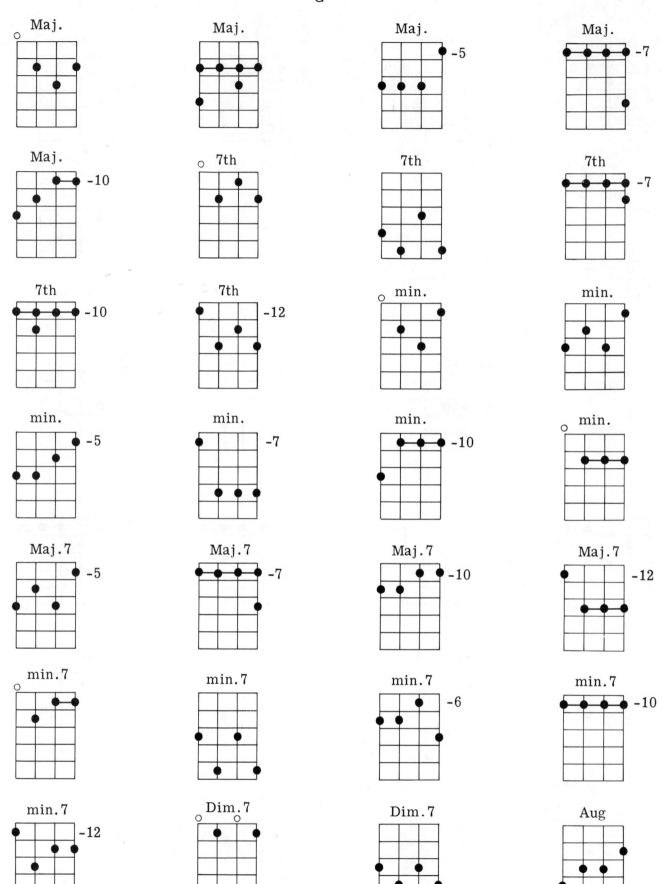

A♭ / G♯

Maj.	Maj.	Maj.	Maj.
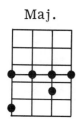	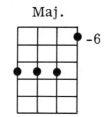 −6	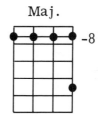 −8	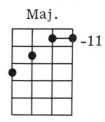 −11

7th	7th	7th	7th
	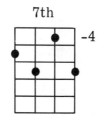 −4	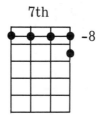 −8	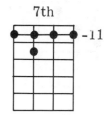 −11

min.	min.	min.	min.
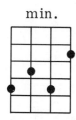	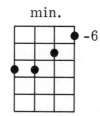 −6	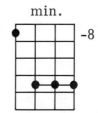 −8	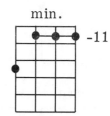 −11

Maj.7	Maj.7	Maj.7	Maj.7
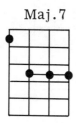	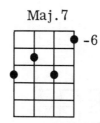 −6	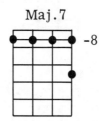 −8	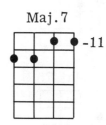 −11

min.7	min.7	min.7	min.7
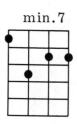	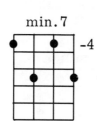 −4	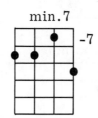 −7	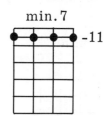 −11

Dim.	Aug.
	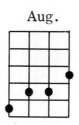

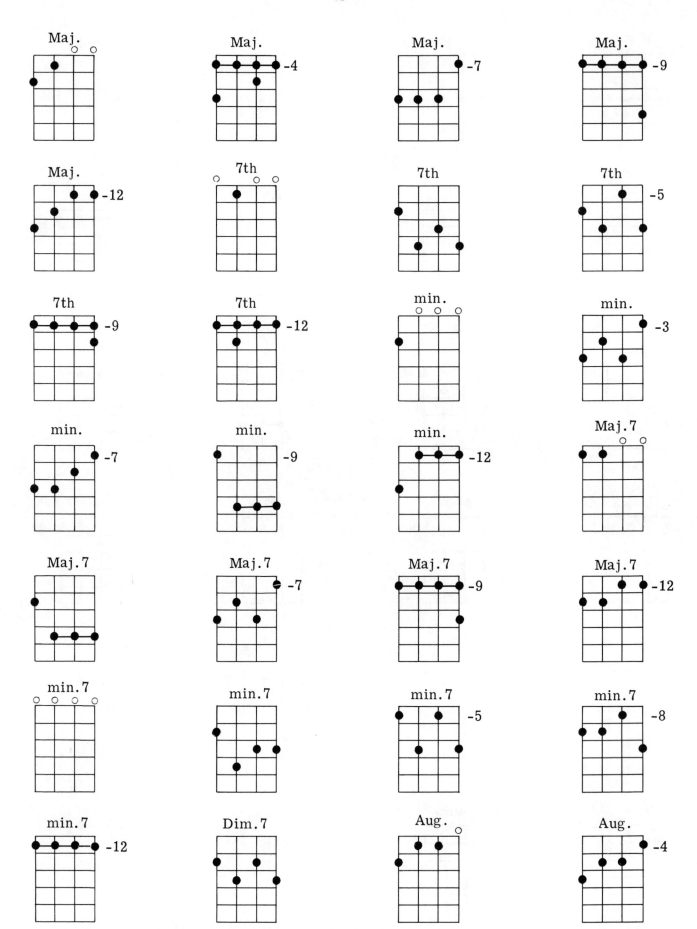

Maj.

Maj.
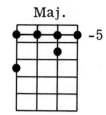
−5

Maj.
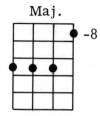
−8

Maj.
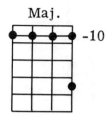
−10

7th
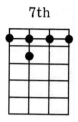

7th
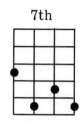

7th
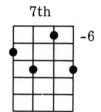
−6

7th
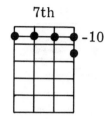
−10

min.
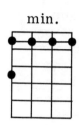

min.
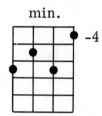
−4

min.
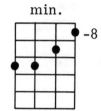
−8

min.
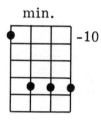
−10

Maj.7
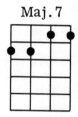

Maj.7
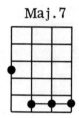

Maj.7
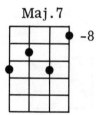
−8

Maj.7
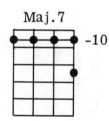
−10

min.7

min.7
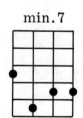

min.7
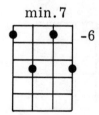
−6

min.7
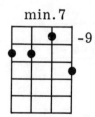
−9

Dim.7
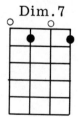

Dim.7
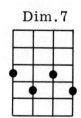

Aug.

B

Maj.
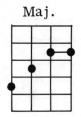

Maj. -6
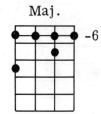

Maj. -9
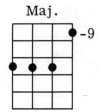

Maj. -11
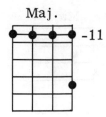

7th

7th -4
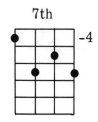

7th -7
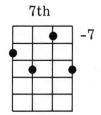

7th -11
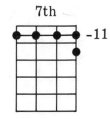

min.
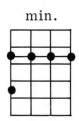

min. -5
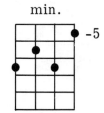

min. -9
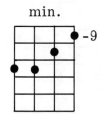

min. -11
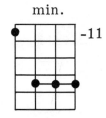

Maj.7
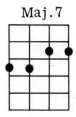

Maj.7 -4
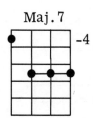

Maj.7 -9
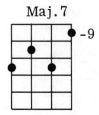

Maj.7 -11
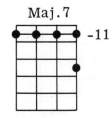

min.7
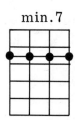

min.7 -4
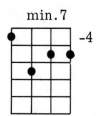

min.7 -7
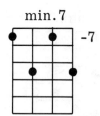

min.7 -10
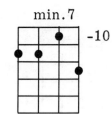

Dim.7
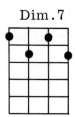

Aug.
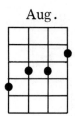

AFTERWORD

Well that's it. After working through the songs presented here, it should be clear that the ukulele is capable of much more than rhythmic strums. In fact the instrument's capabilities are determined by the player's ability and imagination more than any intrinsic limitations. Listen to the modern masters of the instrument, such a Herb Ohta, Eddie Kamae, Peter Moon and others to see how much more can be done. Then do it, and be the next master.

ALPHABETICAL LISTING OF SONGS

Akahi Hoi	91	Luana's Dance	83
Alekoki	88	Makalapua Version I	81
Alika	89	Makalapua Version II	82
Aloha No Wau I Ko Maka	56	Manuela Boy	25
Aloha Oe	73	Manu Oo	65
Betsy's Tune	62	Maui No Ka Oe	34
Friend's Lullaby	76	Mauna Kea	44
Halona	58	Maunawili	23
Hame Pila	57	Moani Ke Ala	80
Hawaii Ponoi	53	My Honolulu Hula Girl	26
He Aloha No Kauiki	28	Nuuanu Waipuna	71
Heeia	61	Paahana	41
Hiilawe	59	Pauahi O Kalani	85
Hilo March	24	Pua Sadinia	79
Honesakala	32	Pulupe Nei Ili I Ke Anu	70
Hula For Ken	48	Sakura	94
Hula O Makee	72	Sunny Moana	30
Hanohano Hanalei	66	Sweet Lei Lehua	63
Ipo's Song	29	Sweet Lei Mamo	46
Koni Au I Ka Wai	22	Think Palm Trees	51
Kuu Ipo I Ka Hee Pue One	38	This Pretty Ukulele	42
Kuwili	37	Ua Like No A Like	49
Lei Nani	45	Violeta	84
Lei Ohaoha	68	Waialae	90
Lei Ohu	50	Waltz For My Dear	36
Lei Poni Moi	92	Wiliwili Wai	78
Liliu E	35		